CRE▲TIVE
HOMEOWNER®

W9-AXY-398

trim
step-by-step projects

CREATIVE HOMEOWNER®, Upper Saddle River, New Jersey

VP, Editorial Director: Timothy O. Bakke
Production Manager: Kimberly H. Vivas

Author: Mark Feirer
Editor: Fran J. Donegan
Assistant Editor/Photo Researcher: Sharon Ranftle
Assistant Editor: Jennifer Ramcke

Senior Designer: David Geer
Cover: Gary David Gold (photography), Clarke Barre (design)

Current Printing (last digit)
10 9 8 7 6 5 4 3

Smart Guide: Trim
Library of Congress Control Number: 2002109960
ISBN: 1-58011-140-8

CREATIVE HOMEOWNER®
A Division of Federal Marketing Corp.
24 Park Way
Upper Saddle River, NJ 07458
www.creativehomeowner.com

Metric Conversion

Length

1 inch	25.4 mm
1 foot	0.3048 m
1 yard	0.9144 m
1 mile	1.61 km

Area

1 square inch	645 mm^2
1 square foot	0.0929 m^2
1 square yard	0.8361 m^2
1 acre	4046.86 m^2
1 square mile	2.59 km^2

Volume

1 cubic inch	16.3870 cm^3
1 cubic foot	0.03 m^3
1 cubic yard	0.77 m^3

Common Lumber Equivalents

Sizes: Metric cross sections are so close to their U.S. sizes, as noted below, that for most purposes they may be considered equivalents.

Dimensional lumber		
	1 × 2	19 × 38 mm
	1 × 4	19 × 89 mm
	2 × 2	38 × 38 mm
	2 × 4	38 × 89 mm
	2 × 6	38 × 140 mm
	2 × 8	38 × 184 mm
	2 × 10	38 × 235 mm
	2 × 12	38 × 286 mm

Capacity

1 fluid ounce	29.57 mL
1 pint	473.18 mL
1 quart	1.14 L
1 gallon	3.79 L

Weight

1 ounce	28.35g
1 pound	0.45kg

Temperature

Fahrenheit = Celsius × 1.8 + 32
Celsius = Fahrenheit − 32 × ⁵⁄₉

Nail Size & Length

Penny Size	Nail Length
2d	1"
3d	1¼"
4d	1½"
5d	1¾"
6d	2"
7d	2¼"
8d	2½"
9d	2¾"
10d	3"
12d	3¼"
16d	3½"

Photo Credits

page 1: Gary David Gold, CH **page 3:** *top* courtesy of Style Solutions; *top middle, bottom middle & bottom* Gary David Gold, CH **page 5:** *top left* courtesy of Style Solutions; *top middle* Mark Lohman; *top right* courtesy of Georgia-Pacific; *bottom right* courtesy of Springs Window Fashions & Nanik Shutters; *bottom left* Mark Lohman **page 21:** *all* Gary David Gold, CH **page 29:** *top left* Gary David Gold, CH; *top right* courtesy of York Wallcoverings; *bottom right* Gary David Gold, CH; *bottom left* www.davidduncanlivingston.com **page 53:** *top left, top middle, bottom right & bottom left* Gary David Gold, CH; *top right* courtesy of Style Solutions **page 71:** *top left* Mark Lohman; *top right, bottom right & bottom left* Gary David Gold, CH

contents

safety first

Though all the designs and methods in this book have been reviewed for safety, it is not possible to overstate the importance of using the safest construction methods possible. What follows are reminders; some do's and don'ts of basic carpentry. They are not substitutes for your own common sense.

- *Always* use caution, care, and good judgment when following the procedures described in this book.

- *Always* be sure that the electrical setup is safe; be sure that no circuit is overloaded and that all power tools and electrical outlets are properly grounded. Do not use power tools in wet locations.

- *Always* read container labels on paints, solvents, and other products; provide ventilation, and observe all other warnings.

- *Always* read the manufacturer's instructions for using a tool, especially the warnings.

- *Always* use hold-downs and push sticks whenever possible when working on a table saw. Avoid working short pieces if you can.

- *Always* remove the key from any drill chuck (portable or press) before starting the drill.

- *Always* pay deliberate attention to how a tool works so that you can avoid being injured.

- *Always* know the limitations of your tools. Do not try to force them to do what they were not designed to do.

- *Always* make sure that any adjustment is locked before proceeding. For example, always check the rip fence on a table saw or the bevel adjustment on a portable saw before starting to work.

- *Always* clamp small pieces firmly to a bench or other work surface when using a power tool on them.

- *Always* wear the appropriate rubber or work gloves when handling chemicals, moving or stacking lumber, or doing heavy construction.

- *Always* wear a disposable face mask when you create dust by sawing or sanding. Use a special filtering respirator when working with toxic substances and solvents.

- *Always* wear eye protection, especially when using power tools or striking metal on metal or concrete; a chip can fly off, for example, when chiseling concrete.

- *Always* be aware that there is seldom enough time for your body's reflexes to save you from injury from a power tool in a dangerous situation; everything happens too fast. Be *alert!*

- *Always* keep your hands away from the business ends of blades, cutters, and bits.

- *Always* hold a circular saw firmly, usually with both hands so that you know where they are.

- *Always* use a drill with an auxiliary handle to control the torque when large-size bits are used.

- *Always* check your local building codes when planning new construction. The codes are intended to protect public safety and should be observed to the letter.

- *Never* work with power tools when you are tired or under the influence of alcohol or drugs.

- *Never* cut tiny pieces of wood or pipe using a power saw. Cut small pieces off larger pieces.

- *Never* change a saw blade or a drill or router bit unless the power cord is unplugged. Do not depend on the switch being off; you might accidentally hit it.

- *Never* work in insufficient lighting.

- *Never* work while wearing loose clothing, hanging hair, open cuffs, or jewelry.

- *Never* work with dull tools. Have them sharpened, or learn how to sharpen them yourself.

- *Never* use a power tool on a work-piece—large or small—that is not firmly supported.

- *Never* saw a workpiece that spans a large distance between horses without close support on each side of the cut; the piece can bend, closing on and jamming the blade, causing saw kickback.

- *Never* support a workpiece from underneath with your leg or other part of your body when sawing.

- *Never* carry sharp or pointed tools, such as utility knives, awls, or chisels, in your pocket. If you want to carry such tools, use a special-purpose tool belt with leather pockets and holders.

chapter 1

selecting trim

Decorative Trim

Trim comes in a variety of shapes, sizes, and species of wood. You will often find the words "trim" and "molding" used interchangeably. "Trim" is used as a general description of any wood in a house that isn't structural lumber—base, casing, crown molding, chair rail, and the like. The professional who traditionally installs all this material is called a trim carpenter or finish carpenter. "Molding" (sometimes spelled moulding) is a term that refers specifically to strips of material, usually wood, that have been cut, shaped, or embossed in some way to create a decorative effect. Molding includes everything from simple quarter-rounds to elaborate crown molding.

Flat Trim

Shaped Trim (Molding)

Decorative Trim. Trim comes in an endless variety of configurations.

Nailing Trim to the Wall

Trim comes in such a wide variety of profiles and thicknesses that it is difficult to give universal nailing recommendations. In general, however, nails should penetrate into solid framing. That means the nail should be long enough to go through the molding, through the drywall or plaster, and into the framing securely. For outdoor work, all nails should be hot-dipped galvanized; indoors, uncoated steel nails are best.

To install large molding—crown, cove, base, and chair rail—drive two finishing nails into each stud. One nail should be about ½-inch from the bottom edge, the other ½-inch from the top. Small molding like base cap and quarter round needs only one nail per stud. It's a good idea to keep three sizes of finishing nails on hand: 4d, 6d, and 8d. When nailing near the end of a run of molding, predrill the nailholes to keep the wood from splitting and to make sure that the nail goes where you want it to. Use a $\frac{5}{64}$-inch bit for 4d nails, a $\frac{3}{32}$-inch bit for 6d nails, and a $\frac{7}{64}$-inch bit for 8d nails.

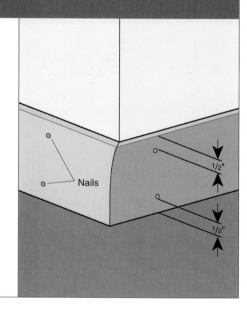

Nails

½"

½"

Purposes of Trim

To properly incorporate trim into the design of a house, you should consider both decorative and functional details. Though trim is most often used decoratively, it is hardly without utility. In fact, trim can be essential to preserving the structural integrity of a house by blocking the passage of water or protecting a surface against mechanical damage.

Used as a Barrier. Trim around the outside of a window or door, for example, bridges the gap between the jamb and sheathing to keep water out, while eave trim closes the gap between the roof and wall. Inside the house, base protects

Used as a Barrier. (A) Trim, or molding, is often used to cover the inevitable gap where two or more materials meet. Door trim and window trim are the most common example of this. **(B)** This detail of crown molding and frieze board shows how trim can be combined in a decorative detail that is also functional. **(C)** One reason baseboard is used to protect the lower portion of walls becomes clear when you consider baseboard's other name: mopboard. **(D)** Plywood makes good shelf material, but the exposed layers of veneer would soon become damaged if they were not covered with solid wood shelf edging.

walls just as shelf trim protects the edges of shelving.

Used as a Cover-up. Trim can minimize problems caused by the natural movement of wood. Wood is inherently an unstable material; exposed to water or humidity it will swell; then it will shrink as heat or dry air drives the moisture out. Over time, this movement forms gaps that are more than unsightly: they can also collect dirt and debris. The proper application of trim won't stop the wood from moving, but it can minimize the problems that it causes.

Used as a Decoration. When applied to a plain surface such as a flush door, for example, the added pattern and texture of molding can make the door a lot more interesting. Crown molding serves a purely decorative purpose in dressing up the juncture of wall and ceiling, and it draws the eye upward much as a church spire does.

Used as a Cover-up. Install wood flooring with a gap between it and the wall to allow for movement. By nailing the base and shoe into the wall, the flooring is free to move.

Used as a Decoration. An inexpensive flat panel door can be transformed with molding and imagination. This door uses panel molding to mimic a panel door.

Attaching Trim

Trim is found throughout a house, both indoors and outdoors. As a decorative device it is the hallmark of fine construction, but decoration is hardly its only role. One of the most common uses of trim is to conceal the gap that inevitably occurs **(A)** between like materials that are prone to seasonal shrinkage and expansion, or **(B)** between disparate materials.

Design Principles

Trim comes in a considerable array of sizes and shapes, most of which can be used in many ways. Here are some guidelines for choosing patterns and profiles.

Stick with One Style. It is a rare room that can handle a smorgasbord of trim styles, so pick a style and stick with it. If you are adding trim to an existing room, match the existing trim. Take a few samples to the lumberyard to ensure a match—you might find a couple of lengths stashed in your attic or tucked away in your garage. If you're combining trim styles, work with compatible shapes.

Watch the Intersections. In any room, various elements of trim or molding will intersect each other, such as where baseboard meets a door casing. The relative thicknesses and widths will determine whether the elements meet harmoniously or awkwardly. Before you settle on a collection of trim, get samples

Various Base Treatments

Beveled-Edge Base

Base Shoe

Clamshell Base

Clamshell Stop

Ogee Base

1"x1¼" Ogee Molding

Colonial Base

Ogee Panel Molding

Cove Molding

Cove Molding

3" Flat Stock

Bed Molding

1"x1½" Ogee Molding

Stick with One Style. Even though these bases were built up using individual pieces, the profiles of each element are compatible with others in the same assembly.

(scraps will suffice) so that you can examine the intersections in advance.

Think "Finishes" before Finishing.
Staining trim usually makes it stand out; painting it to match surrounding surfaces helps it to blend in. Trim that contrasts with surrounding surfaces emphasizes its linear nature. Painted trim allows a greater margin of error; you can fill small gaps before you paint. Stained or clear-finished trim, on the other hand, will point out every mistake.

Watch the Intersections. (A) Here the outside edge of the door casing is thicker than the baseboard, so the two intersect nicely. If the reverse was true, the end grain of the baseboard would be exposed and form a rather clumsy-looking detail. **(B)** In this case, the flat trim and quarter-round used to cap a woodstove platform butts nicely into the side of the baseboard. If the quarter-round was instead an ogee, it might be an even better match. **(C)** These two trim elements don't even come close to blending nicely. A better solution would be to run square trim alongside the fireplace all the way to the floor, then butt the baseboard into it. **(D)** The corner guard meets the underside of the wainscoting cap in tolerable fashion. It meets the baseboard in a much more visible location, however, and is much clumsier in appearance.

Avoid Awkward Applications.

When it comes to applying trim to angled features, such as sloped ceilings, the work gets complicated in a hurry—you'll have to make some tricky compound-angle cuts. Even then, the results may not look quite right, so it may be best to save your trimwork for other parts of the room.

Use Classic Applications. Builders in ancient Greece (who originated many of the profiles upon which modern moldings are based) realized that decorative moldings looked best when they were viewed head on. In this way, shadows wouldn't obscure the molding.

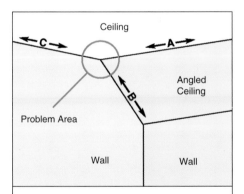

Think "Finishes" before Finishing.
You can use paintable caulk to hide any gaps in trim that will be painted. This is particularly useful where trim is being installed on a wall that's not perfectly flat.

Avoid Awkward Applications.
An intersection like this is best left untrimmed. The intersecting ceiling planes would make the application of crown molding quite difficult. The crown couldn't follow the ceiling line "A" because the obtuse angle following ceiling line "B" would result in an awkward intersection with any trim along line "C."

Use Classic Applications.
Trim should appear correct to the eye at a normal stance. Trim pieces toward the top of a wall generally angle downward, while those at the bottom usually have a profile that is heavier at the bottom than at the top, and tend to angle upward.

Species & Grades of Trim

Trim is available in various species of softwoods. The most commonly available are fir, pine, hemlock/fir, and spruce, though availability varies considerably from region to region. Softwoods are easy to cut, relatively inexpensive, suitable for use outdoors, and readily stained or painted. When it comes to hardwood, most home centers and lumberyards carry only oak. Oak is more difficult to work with and considerably more expensive than any of the softwoods. It is rarely used for outdoor trim, but it is more attractive than softwoods and is generally used where work is to be stained or left natural.

Grading is a way of distinguishing one piece of wood from another in terms of its quality and its suitability for a particular purpose. It also has a considerable effect on the cost of wood. In order to control your costs, always purchase wood in the grade most suitable for the work you are doing. Buying a higher quality than you need entails needless expense.

The grading of trim is quite complicated, and terms used to describe various grades often vary from region to region. In general, however, trim is divided into appearance grades and general-purpose grades. Each of these grades is further divided into numerous subcategories. Appearance grades are most suited to the high-quality finish uses, particularly indoors (though you may find that the best of the general-purpose boards will suit your needs as well). In addition, you may see trim stock referred to by the term "S4S" (surfaced four sides). This means both faces and both edges have been planed smooth.

The kinds of trim you'll find in most home centers are divided into two basic grades: clear and paint-grade. Clear trim is made from solid lengths of high-quality wood and has few

Species & Grades of Trim. Clear and paint-grade trim is generally available; veneered trim is available in some areas of the country. Rigid polyurethane trim is a popular alternative to wood.

visible defects. This premium product can be painted or stained. Paint-grade trim consists of many small pieces of wood joined together into one long piece using adhesives and interlocking joinery. This material is sometimes called "finger-jointed" stock, after the joinery method used to connect the pieces. The pieces themselves are good-quality wood, but neighboring pieces often vary a great deal in color and grain. These differences are concealed when the trim is painted, however, making the finished product virtually indistinguishable from clear trim. As you might expect, paint-grade trim is less expensive than clear trim.

There is another grade of trim worth noting. Known by various trade names, it is essentially finger-jointed wood stock wrapped either with solid-wood veneer or wood-grained vinyl. Both of these hybrid products can be cut with standard woodworking tools and are nailed in place just

like standard trim. However, you must take particular care not to damage the thin outer layer during installation.

Wood isn't the only material used for trim, however. Some lumberyards carry trim made entirely of rigid furniture-grade polyurethane that has a paintable coating. The molding comes in very detailed, classically-inspired profiles that would be difficult and costly to reproduce in wood. Rigid polyurethane is lightweight and very stable, and cuts can be made with a hand saw. The material is typically installed using a proprietary construction adhesive, with a few small nails here and there to hold lengths in place while the adhesive cures. Once painted, the molding is difficult to distinguish from solid wood. Polyurethane molding usually costs more than wood molding, but it will take a lot less time to install detailed profiles that you would have to build up with wood.

Guidelines for Buying Trim

For a relatively small project—trimming a single window, perhaps—all you have to do is go to the lumberyard, buy a length or two of casing, then come home to install it. But large jobs are different; any new room could well require base, chair rail, ceiling molding, base shoe, and casings for doors and windows. You will get the best price, and save yourself many trips to the supplier, if you purchase all of your trim at the same time.

Because of the variations in grading around the country, it's best to visit your local supplier before ordering trim. Ask to see samples of various grades—many suppliers keep samples on hand just for this purpose. Be sure to describe what you plan to do with the wood and how you intend to finish it; the supplier can often recommend less-expensive grades that will perform very well.

Checking for Deformities. The problems that plague framing lumber, such as warping and twisting, affect trim to a lesser extent. This is because trim is carefully dried before shipping, whereas lumber is often shipped "green." However, you should still pick material with care in order to identify any problems before you will have to deal with them. First, sight down the length of the wood; this will make it easy to see twisted or bowed stock. Usually a gradual bow in trim won't be much of a problem—the wood is thin enough to straighten out against the wall as you nail it into place. Then scrutinize the trim for splits or any other damage.

Choosing the Stock. Because trim comes in lengths of 8 to 16 feet, you should rarely need more than one piece to trim a given wall. If you're on a tight budget, though, shorter pieces sometimes cost less than longer ones. The techniques used to

Guidelines for Buying Trim. Sight down the length of a piece of trim to determine whether it is straight. A slight bow is okay, but any twist will cause problems during installation.

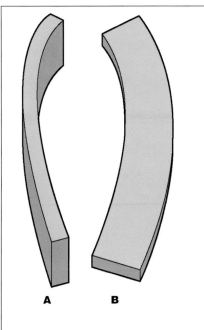

Checking for Deformities. A trim board bowed across its thickness **(A)** may be usable, but a board bowed even slightly across its width **(B)** will be difficult to work with.

mill moldings aren't perfect, so check any moldings that you buy for fractional differences in width and thickness. Whenever possible, buy all of the molding for a project at one time to minimize any variations. Even a small variation in width can make an otherwise perfect joint look clumsy.

Storage Tips

Proper storage cannot be overemphasized. Trim should always be stored indoors, preferably in the same space in which it will be installed. This allows it to acclimate to the moisture levels present in the room. Keep trim away from all masonry walls and floors (particularly floors). These surfaces will wick harmful moisture into the house from the outside, and it's the moisture that can cause damage to the trim. Badly warped trim is unusable, good only for the scrap heap.

During the course of the project, make it a point to save any scrap trim that is 6 inches in length or more until the end of the job. You will often need some scraps to experiment on, such as when setting up test cuts. Also, you'll find that shorter pieces are useful as stock from which to cut small pieces called "mitered returns." (See "Mitered Returns," page 33.) Even after the job is complete, you should still save some scraps—they may come in handy later if you have to make unforeseen repairs.

Estimating Trim Stock. Trim stock typically comes in lengths from 8 to 16 feet, but you can usually get shorter lengths if you ask (though you may have to pay extra if the lumberyard has to cut trim for you). Simply measure the amount you'll need, add about 10 percent to account for waste, and you're in business. Purchase the long- est lengths of stock that you can transport; this will give you the most flexibility when it's time to cut the material to fit.

To figure out how much you'll need, measure each wall and round up the number to the next foot. In other words, a 5-foot 6-inch wall requires a 6-foot length of trim. To allow for cutting waste, each piece of trim for the wall should be longer than the wall it will cover. If the wall is almost the length of a full piece, buy the next longest length. That means ordering 8-foot lengths of trim for a wall whose length is within an inch or two of 6 feet.

Estimating Plain Stock. Finished lumber typically comes in the widths shown in the chart below. The nominal size is what you would ask for; the "actual" size is what it measures.

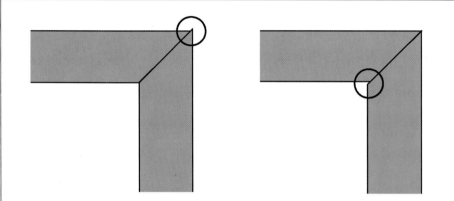

Choosing the Stock. A difference in width between two lengths of casing will cause problems even if the joint between them is perfect. On the left the "horn" resulting from differing casing widths can be sanded down. On the right, however, there's not much you can do about the unsightly gap.

Finished Lumber Sizes	
Nominal size (in inches)	Actual size (in inches)
1x2	3/4 x 1 1/2
1x3	3/4 x 2 1/2
1x4	3/4 x 3 1/2
1x6	3/4 x 5 1/2
1x8	3/4 x 7 1/4
1x10	3/4 x 9 1/4
1x12	3/4 x 11 1/4

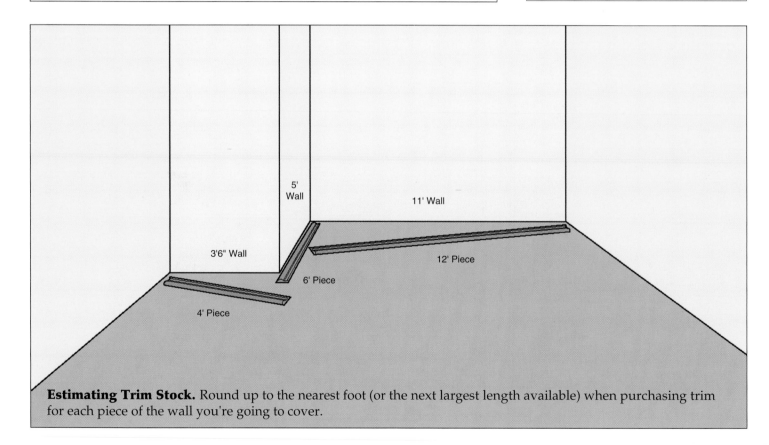

5'
Wall

11' Wall

3'6" Wall

12' Piece

6' Piece

4' Piece

Estimating Trim Stock. Round up to the nearest foot (or the next largest length available) when purchasing trim for each piece of the wall you're going to cover.

Types of Molding

You will find that the molding bins are stuffed with every conceivable shape or profile of molding, and nearly every one of them is available in several dimensions.

Base Trim. Base protects the lower portion of the walls and covers any gaps between the wall and the floor. Base shoe molding is used to conceal any variation between the floor and the base bottom. It is also used to cover edges of sheet vinyl flooring (when installed without first removing the base).

Ceiling Molding. Cove covers the inside corners between sheets of paneling. It is also used for built-up crown molding. Crown molding can

Base Molding. Base protects the bottoms of walls, and base shoe covers the joint between base and floor.

Typical Cove Molding

Typical Crown Molding

Ceiling Molding. At the intersection of the wall and ceiling, cove or crown molding is installed.

be used for dramatic effect at the juncture of walls and ceilings.

Wall Molding. Wainscot cap can be used to cover the exposed end grain on solid-wood wainscoting or to finish off the top of flat baseboards. Chair rail is installed at the height that protects walls from being damaged by chair backs. It is also used to cover the edges of wallpaper wainscoting. Picture molding is used in conjunction with metal hooks for hanging paintings. It eliminates the need to put holes in the wall. Corner molding protects the outside corners of drywall or plaster in high-traffic areas.

Casing. Casing conceals the gap between jambs and the surrounding wall. Common types of casing

Wall Molding. (Top) Wainscot cap and chair rail are often used to bridge differences between materials on a wall. (Bottom left) Corner molding protects vulnerable corners from damage. (Bottom right) Picture molding allows pictures to be added, moved, and removed without marring wall surfaces.

include ranch, clamshell, and colonial. Mullion casing is used as the center trim between two or more closely spaced windows. Be sure it is compatible with the window casing in style and thickness. If you don't find a casing style that you like, you can make your own out of flat trim stock. Even a pair of ⅛-inch deep kerfs, cut lengthwise in the stock on a table saw, can add a dramatic detail.

Other. Back band molding can be used to give the outer edges of flat casing a more decorative profile. It can also be used as a base cap or even as inexpensive stock for framing small artwork. Shelf edging covers the exposed edges of plywood or particleboard casework and shelving. This is an inexpensive way to give manufactured material the look of solid wood.

Casing. Window and door casing are among the most important trim elements for setting the style of a room.

Other. Varieties of trim can be combined—back band surrounds flat casing. Shelf edging is also used on casework.

Making Your Own Molding

While your local lumberyard probably stocks any molding profile you want in softwood or oak, you'll have a hard time finding moldings in walnut, cherry, or any other hardwood species you have in mind. But cherry stain doesn't really look like cherry wood, and no matter what stain you put on oak, the grain will never look like walnut. For the real thing, you'll need to take out the router.

These days router bits are available in hundreds of decorative shapes. You can put a decorative edge on a piece of stock and use it as is. Or to make thin moldings, you can rip the decorative edge off the board and rout the board again, repeating this process so that one board serves as rough stock for several lengths of molding. By varying the depth of cut and com-bining different bits, even more profiles are possible.

Before using any router to cut custom molding profiles, be sure that you know how to use the tool. Also remember that routers generate a great deal of sawdust and are very loud; protect your eyes and your hearing. Carbide-tipped router bits are more expensive than steel bits, but they keep a sharp edge longer and cut cleanly through nearly any wood.

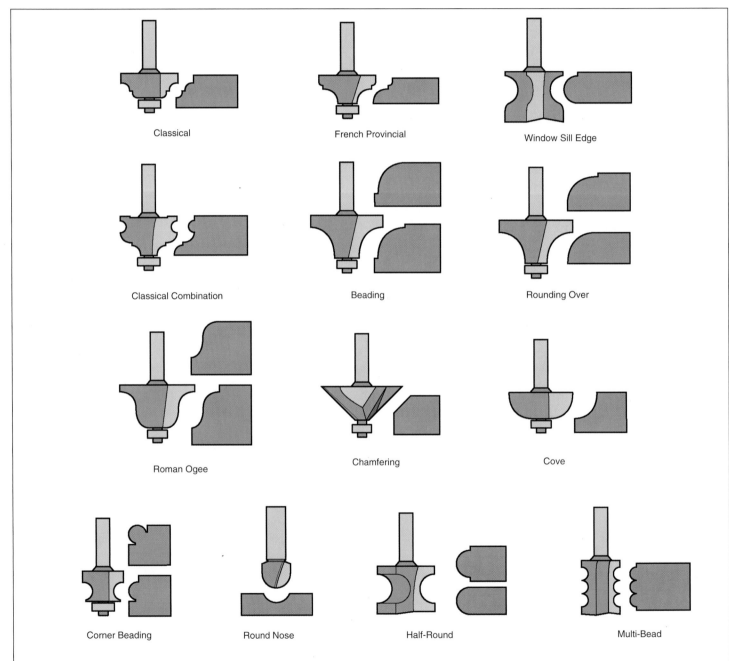

Classical

French Provincial

Window Sill Edge

Classical Combination

Beading

Rounding Over

Roman Ogee

Chamfering

Cove

Corner Beading

Round Nose

Half-Round

Multi-Bead

Making Your Own Molding. These are just a few of the router bits available and the profiles they produce.

Cutting Custom Profiles

1 **Securing the Stock.** First examine the board for knots, cracks, and other imperfections that would interfere with the cut. Tight knots that are small usually won't cause a problem, but you should avoid large or loose knots. Always clamp the stock to a solid surface so that you can keep both hands on the router itself.

2 **Adjusting the Depth of Cut.** With the router unplugged and resting on top of the board, sight along the edge of the board. Adjust the height of the router bit, plug the router in, and make a trial cut. (If you use scrap stock for this, it should be the same thickness as the final stock.)

3 **Making the Cut.** The router bit will spin clockwise. Guide it along the edge of the board as shown; the direction in which you work is important. Experiment with the rate of feed: too fast and you may damage the molding; too slow and the bit may leave burn marks on the wood. Multiple light passes will produce the cleanest edge with a minimum of burning.

4 **Removing the Molding.** If you are making molding, cut the routed edge from the board, set it aside, and then rout the fresh edge. You can continue to do this as long as you can safely clamp the stock in place while routing and safely cut it off on the table saw.

1 The board should be clamped to a workbench in at least two places to keep it from slipping. Make sure that the clamps are well away from the edge to be cut, otherwise they will interfere with the router.

2 You may have to adjust the depth of the bit several times before you get exactly the cut you want.

3 Moving the router as shown here improves your control, and thus the safety of the operation.

4 Cut the molded edge free using a table saw. The safest way is to place the unmolded edge of the board against the saw's fence, rather than trapping the slender molding between blade and fence.

Assembling Custom Profiles

If a local supplier has a good selection of moldings, ask for some scraps and experiment with various combinations. When you find a suitable combination, you can either nail it in place piece by piece or nail all of the pieces together into lengths, and then install the assembly just as you would any other molding. Once installed and painted, it will look just like solid stock. Get a price estimate on the molding, though, before you load up on enough of it to do a room; molding can be expensive, built-up molding even more so.

Built-Up Crown Molding

Cove

Base

Crown

Base

Dentil

Crown

Crown

Cove

Built-Up Chair Rail

Torus or Astragal

Flat Chair Rail

Base Caps

Cove

Flat Trim

Cove

Built-Up Casing

Colonial Casing

Back Band

Colonial Base

Base Cap

Flat Chair Rail

Half Rounds

Assembling Custom Profiles. Built-up moldings work well as crown, chair rail, and casing.

tools & more

Tools

To install trim you will need some basic tools. At the very least, you'll need a measuring tape, hammer, hand saw, miter box, and some nail sets, along with a good, sharp pencil. These tools are widely available and relatively inexpensive.

Purchase additional tools as you need them. Power tools can improve the accuracy and speed of your work. Hand tools are perfectly suitable, however, particularly if you work with trim only occasionally.

Tools

Power Miter Saw

Sanding Block

Drill

Miter Box

Router

Putty Knife

Measuring Tape

Combination Square

Block Plane

Back Saw

Nippers

Claw Hammer

Cat's Paw

Nail Set

Hand Saw

Pry Bar

9" Torpedo Level

Pencil

Coping Saw

Level

Sliding T-Bevel

Framing Square

Glue Gun

Random Orbital Sander

Chinese Bristle Paintbrush

Handle

Trim Roller

3" Touch-Up Roller

Chinese Bristle Paintbrush

Finishing Sander

Chisel-Edge Paintbrush

Palm Sander

Trim Paintbrush

Plate Joiner

Phillips Screwdriver

Step Stool

Trim Paintbrush

Surform Tool

Flat-Bladed Screwdriver

Using a Measuring Tape

A measuring tape is a simple device, but it is easy to use improperly. Here are some tips for getting the best results with this important tool.

Checking for Accuracy. Any measuring tape can be damaged if dropped, so check your tape periodically for accuracy. (Even a new one should be checked before you use it for the first time.) The hook at the end of the blade slides back and forth just enough to account for its own thickness when you take inside or outside measurements; a bent hook or one that does not slide will give you inaccurate measurements. To check its accuracy, hook the tape on the edge of a board and make a mark at the 12-inch line. Now measure the same distance using only the graduated marks printed on the tape itself. Hold the 1-inch mark on the edge of the board, and then measure out to your previous mark: it should fall exactly at the number 13. Carpenters sometimes call measuring in this way "burning an inch." If the measurements don't match, carefully bend the hook as needed until they do.

Making Measurements. To ensure an accurate measurement, always be sure that the tape is flat against the surface that you're measuring. This is especially important when measuring long, flexible pieces of trim.

If you have to make a long inside measurement (the distance between two opposite walls, for example), hook the tape on a small finishing nail tapped into the corner. The small hole remaining after you remove the nail will rarely be noticed.

Using the Small Slot. Have you ever looked at the hook of a measuring tape and wondered what the small slot is for? It allows you to hook the tape on the head of a common nail and single-handedly make long measurements. With the nail serving as a pivot point, you can also use the tape to draw circles.

Maintenance & Care. A spring-loaded tape returns to its case quickly, but you should never let it snap back at full speed because this will eventually break the end of the tape. Instead, hold a finger under the tape so you can slow it down as it retracts. Periodically wipe dirt and grime off of the tape, especially around the hook. If the tape itself breaks, you may be able to purchase a replacement cartridge for less than the cost of an entire new measuring tape.

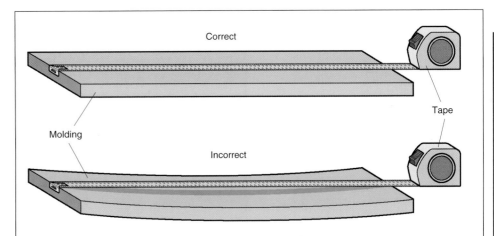

Making Measurements. Always measure molding with the tape flat against the wood along its entire length. Any gap between tape and wood will lead to inaccurate measurements.

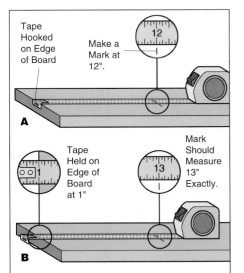

Checking for Accuracy. Test the accuracy of a measuring tape by measuring to a mark both **(A)** with and **(B)** without using the hook. They should match.

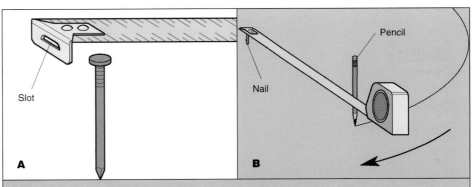

Using the Small Slot. (A) The slot in the end of a measuring tape will fit over the head of a common nail to keep the tape from slipping as you measure away from the nail. **(B)** To lay out a rough circle, nail into a surface, hook the tape on the nail, then hold a pencil against the tape and swing a series of arcs.

Using a Hammer

A hammer can cause serious injury if used improperly. But it is an indispensible tool if used properly when installing trim.

Saving Time. You'll move around the room a lot while installing trim. Much of your time will be spent looking for your hammer unless you keep it ready at your side. You can purchase a webbed belt with a leather pad and metal hanger for the hammer, or simply slip the hammer into the loop of an inexpensive canvas nail apron or leather tool pouch. Either way, your hammer will always be at hand when you need it.

Removing a Nail. Finishing nails have a small head that a hammer can't always hold. It may help to bend the nail slightly so that the claws can get a better grip. If you are working with softwood trim, slip a thin scrap of wood or heavy cardboard under the hammer head before you pull the nail; this will keep the wood fibers from being crushed as you lever the nail out.

Holding Small Nails. Here's how to minimize damage to your fingers when starting small nails. Hold them between two fingers (your fingernails toward the wood) as shown; your fingers will be flat against the wood rather than be angled upward, where the hammer might hit them. When space is really tight, you can hold the nails with needle-nose pliers or even with a piece of cardboard.

Setting a Nail. Nails used for installing trim are shorter and thinner than those used in frame carpentry and will bend easily if you're not careful. To start a nail, hold it in place and tap it lightly a couple of times until it stands by itself. Move your hand away, and tap the nail harder until it is solidly engaged in the wood, then harder still as you drive it into the wood. Stop hammering just as the nailhead reaches the wood; finish the job with a hammer and nail set. This will keep you from dimpling the wood as you drive the nail home.

Saving Time. This configuration is an ideal way to keep a hammer close by when you're not using it. The leather pad can be slipped onto a standard leather belt, too.

Removing a Nail. Protect trim when you pull nails by placing a scrap of wood beneath the hammer's head.

Holding Small Nails. (A) Hold a small nail with your palm up. Once the nail has started, move your hand away. **(B)** Very small nails can be held safely by first pushing them into a scrap of cardboard; hold the cardboard with your fingers well away from potential hammer blows.

Setting a Nail. Hold a nail set by pressing its knurled barrel between your fingers and your thumb. Spread your fingers out slightly to stabilize the nail set, hold it against the nail, and tap the nail until it's just below the surface of the wood.

Using a Power Miter Saw

The easiest and most accurate way to cut molding is with a power miter saw (sometimes called a chop saw because of the downward motion of the blade during cutting). Most power miter saws essentially consist of a circular saw that hangs from a hinged arm over an adjustable table and a stationary fence. The saw pivots left and right to make cuts at various angles. Power miter saws are especially accurate at removing thin slivers of material, which is often required to fit a molding precisely into place. To make the extra-clean cuts needed for trim work, fit the saw with a sharp, 60-tooth to 80-tooth carbide-tipped blade. The primary limitation of power miter saws is that they can't cut wide boards, but most trim is easily accommodated.

Minimizing Problems. Like any power tool, a power miter saw can be dangerous if used improperly. Consult and follow the instructions that come with the saw, and wear both eye and ear protection. In particular, be careful when cutting molding. The pliable nature of thin stock encourages many operators to hold their fingers too close to the blade when cutting—a dangerous habit. Make sure to hold the stock firmly against the fence and flat against the table. The long length and slender profile of moldings such as small coves and base shoe makes them awkward to cut. To minimize problems, support all molding along its entire length.

Making Test Cuts. If you have never used a power miter saw before, make a number of test cuts on scrap stock to get accustomed to the cutting action. Because the saw blade must be aligned with the cut line by eye, it can be hard to get accurate results the first time. Try this approach: pivot the saw down so that the blade's teeth almost touch the wood. (For safety's sake, keep your fingers away from the saw's trigger so you won't start the saw accidentally.) Then use the teeth as a guide to determine exactly where the saw will cut. After pivoting the saw back up and away from the wood, turn on the saw and bring the blade down into the workpiece to make the cut.

Making Test Cuts. Sight down the saw blade and line it up so that its teeth are completely on the "waste" side of the cut line. A proper cut will leave the line intact on the "good" piece, which you can always trim if your cut is slightly long the first time.

Using a Coping Saw

A coping saw has a steel frame and a narrow, flexible blade about 6 inches long, with 12 to 18 teeth per inch. The blade is held in tension between the "jaws" of the frame. Twisting the handle while you cut rotates the blade. This twisting gives the coping saw the ability to cut small-radius curves, making it possible to cut the profile of almost any piece of molding.

Start the coping saw by drawing it back gently over the cut line so that the teeth just barely cut into the wood. Continue to use short, gentle strokes until the blade begins to "track" in the cut, then use longer and firmer strokes.

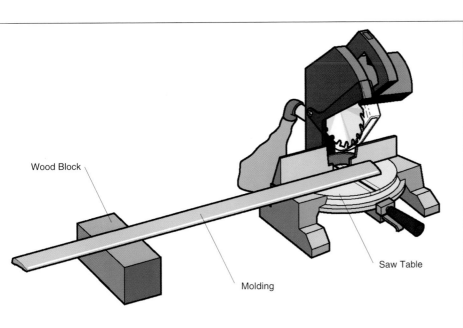

Minimizing Problems. Support molding longer than about 4 ft. with a wood block or some other device.

Using a Miter Box & Backsaw

Even though the power miter saw has become universally popular among professionals, the wooden or plastic miter box still has its place. If you're cutting just a few pieces of trim, for instance, it may be easier to use a handsaw and miter box. And if you have to cut short pieces of trim or if you're at all nervous about using a power saw, a wooden miter box is the best tool to use. Slots in the side of the miter box guide the saw blade and allow you to make crosscuts and 45-degree miter cuts (the cuts you will most often need). You can use the miter box with a backsaw or with a standard carpenter's finishing handsaw, as long as the saw is sharp. The more teeth per inch, the cleaner the cut will be. Sometimes miter boxes are metal and hold the saw in a frame that minimizes wobble. Some of these saws can make compound miters, and some can even handle unusually wide stock. To make a cut, use your free hand to hold the stock firmly against the back of the box. Position your body so that your arm travels in line with the saw. Keep a light but firm grip on the handle, and make the cut using a smooth, easy motion. To keep the cut smooth, don't bear down on the saw; the weight of the saw itself should carry it through the work.

Removing Slivers. Fitting a piece of molding often means shortening it by a fraction of an inch. Such a narrow cut can be difficult to make using a wood miter box because the saw blade tends to wobble off the cut line. To remedy this problem, take some scrap stock and tack it to the bottom of the box at the cut line. The block will serve as a guide to keep the saw blade straight.

Using a Miter Box & Backsaw. Wooden miter boxes are inexpensive, and ideal when cutting short pieces of molding. One advantage of wooden miter boxes is that you can easily attach jigs to help you make a cut. A guide block, for example, allows the saw to remove a sliver from the end of a molding without wandering off the cut.

Using a Spirit Level

A small level (or two) is good to have on hand during trim jobs, though you probably won't use it a lot. Here are some tips for getting the best results with any level.

Reading a Level. First, set the level on the surface you wish to check, making sure the surface is free of sawdust and other debris. Your level may have either one or two sets of lines scribed into the circumference of each vial. Sight straight at the horizontal vial with one eye closed. **(A)** If the bubble is centered between the inner (or only) lines, the surface is level. **(B)** If you can see the lines on the back side of the vial, you're not looking straight at it. If one end of the bubble just touches one of the outer lines, this means the surface is sloping at a rate of ¼ inch per foot (the rate at which plumbers slope drain lines). Some levels have one vial that is angled; when the bubble is centered in this vial, the level is sloping at a 45-degree angle.

Checking Accuracy. An accurate level will read exactly the same if you turn it end for end on the same surface. If it does not and the level is adjustable, loosen the screws that hold each vial in place and adjust the vials until they read accurately.

Nails

Though you may occasionally need to use adhesives when installing trim, nails are the fastener of choice—they're strong, inexpensive, and easily concealed with a dab of wood putty. Three types of nails are commonly used to install trim: finishing nails, casing nails, and brads.

Finishing Nails. This is by far the most common type of nail used to install trim. In fact, it is just about the only nail you need for this kind of work. The nail is characterized by a small, barrel-shaped head and a slender shank. The head, which has a small dimple in the top, is small enough so that you can use a nail set to sink it below the surface of the wood; this technique is called "countersinking." Finishing nails are used whenever the nail must be concealed in the final work.

Casing Nails. A casing nail is similar to a finishing nail, though the underside of its head is tapered. A casing nail has a bit more holding power than a finishing nail of similar length; this is because its diameter is slightly greater than that of a finishing nail. The extra holding power comes in handy when you install exterior casing, which is typically thicker than interior casing. Instead, it is simply driven flush with the surface of the wood and painted over. However, not every supplier carries casing nails.

Brads. Nails shaped like finishing nails but less than 1½ inches long

Nails. Finishing nails and brads have a barrel-shaped head, but the head of a casing nail is more angular.

are called brads. They are used for tacking thin pieces of trim into place.

Buying Nails. Finishing nails and casing nails are available either uncoated or galvanized. Uncoated nails (often labeled "bright" for their shiny steel finish) are suitable for most interior work. Galvanized nails,

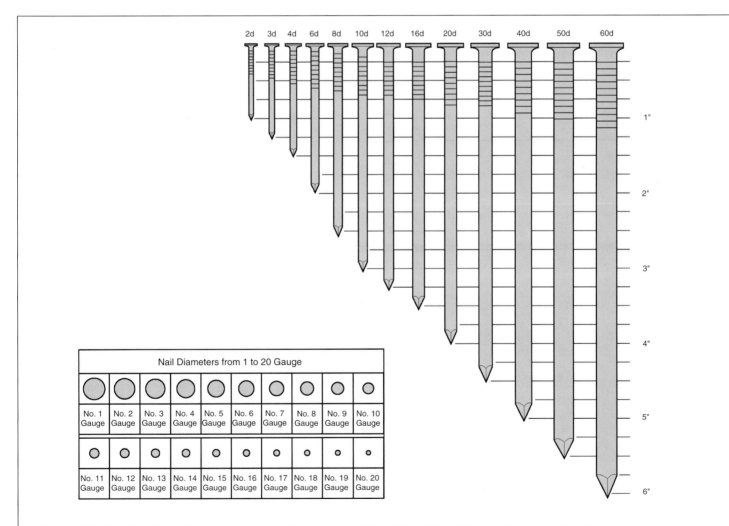

Buying Nails. Use this chart to determine the sizes and lengths of finishing, casing, and standard nails.

on the other hand, are the ones to use outdoors because they are coated with a rust-inhibiting layer of zinc. You can easily recognize galvanized nails by their dull gray color. Sometimes you'll see galvanized nails described further by the type of process used to apply the zinc coating: "hot-dipped" nails generally have a heavier coating of zinc than do "electroplated" nails. Galvanized nails are also appropriate indoors to fasten wood that may come into contact with moisture, such as any trim around a shower stall.

How you buy nails depends partly on where you buy them. The hardware section of a department store, for example, will sell small quantities in plastic packets holding a mere handful of nails each. Nails are cheap, but this is the most expensive way to buy them; use it only when your needs are minimal. At a home supply center or lumberyard, however, you'll also find nails in small boxes holding from 1 to 5 pounds each or in bins that allow you to purchase nails by the pound in whatever quantity you want. The boxes provide a handy way to store unused nails so that they'll be ready for the next project.

Sizes of Nails. Nails were once a precious commodity because each one was made by hand. Modern manufacturing makes nails relatively cheap, but our system of describing the length of nails harkens back to those early days. Nails are given a number, followed by a lowercase letter "d." The "d" represents the word *denarius,* Latin for "penny," which in turn refers to the fact that nails were once categorized by how much it cost to buy 100 of them. These days, however, the "d" represents the length of a nail, not its cost. A 2d nail (pronounced "2 penny"), for example, is 1 inch long, while a 60d nail is 6 inches long. Any nail less than 1 inch long is described by its actual length. You will rarely need a finishing or casing nail longer than 16d (approximately 3 1/2 inches).

Basic Nailing Techniques

Blunt the end of a nail to reduce the chance of splitting the wood.

Nails should penetrate the underlying substrate at least two-thirds the length of the nail.

Nails that line up on the grain of the wood will tend to split it. Stagger nails instead.

Predrill nail holes in hardwood to keep the wood from splitting. If you don't have the correct drill bit, cut the head from a finishing nail and chuck it into a drill.

Nails lubricated with wax will be easier to drive into hardwoods.

installation

Cutting Trim

Chances are you'll have to make at least one cut on every piece of trim you install. Unlike other areas of woodworking, where the joints may be structural, the installation of trim (indoors, anyway) is primarily decorative. That means that you can put your effort into making sure that the installation looks good, with tightly fitting joints and no gaps between the wall and trim. If you can master three basic kinds of cuts, your trim project will be well on its way. The basic types of cuts are:

Crosscut. This is usually the easiest cut for beginners to make. Sometimes called a square cut, it is simply a straight cut that runs across the grain of the wood. The grain of trim runs along the length of the wood, so a typical crosscut is across the width of the wood (90 degrees to its edges).

Coped cut. In some joints, one piece of wood must be cut to form a reverse image of the adjoining piece. The resulting cut may require a series of smaller cuts, each of which can be straight or curved. This is called a coped cut.

Miter cut. Miters are cuts made to join two pieces of wood in a miter joint. Like crosscuts, miter cuts run straight across the grain of the wood, but at an angle other than 90 degrees. Miter cuts of 45 degrees are the most common because two pieces cut at this angle mate to form a 90-degree turn.

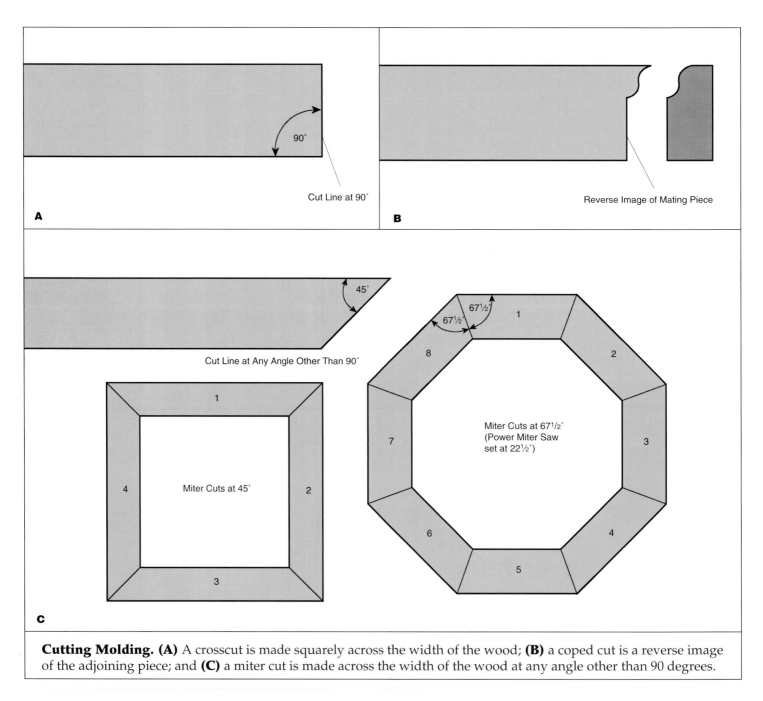

Cutting Molding. (A) A crosscut is made squarely across the width of the wood; **(B)** a coped cut is a reverse image of the adjoining piece; and **(C)** a miter cut is made across the width of the wood at any angle other than 90 degrees.

Woodworking Joinery for Trim

How do you choose which joint to use when two lengths of trim meet? In general, every woodworking joint is a trade-off between strength, appearance, and your ability to use the tools. When installing trim, appearance is usually more important than strength.

Butt Joint. The simple butt joint is a 90-degree cut across the grain of a piece of trim. It's often used where a length of horizontal trim meets a piece of standing (vertical) trim, such as where base meets a door casing. A butt joint is easy to make, though for a tight fit it must be accurately cut. It must meet the vertical trim at a perfect right angle and have a straight, smooth edge that's free of splintering. Any deviation from this will show up as an unsightly gap either at the top or at the bottom of the joint.

Miter Joint. Miters are made by cutting two pieces of molding at an angle and joining them—most commonly at the outside corner where two walls meet or around windows and doors. (See pages 53 to 70.) They're the most visible joints in most rooms, so you should be careful when cutting and fitting them because any deviation from your set angle will be doubled when two cut pieces meet. Miter joints look neat when you first cut them but can sometimes open up with changes in the wood's moisture content. A little glue and a casing nail can be used to close such a gap.

Coped Joint. If you use a miter joint on an inside corner, the joint will open up when you nail the adjoining pieces. It will open further as the wood shrinks with changes in moisture content. The solution is to use a coped joint. This is like a butt joint, except that one piece is cut to fit the profile of the other. Though a coped joint can also open up as the wood shrinks, any gap that results is less obvious than an equal gap in a mitered joint. In other words, a mitered joint accentuates a gap while a coped joint conceals it. Cutting a coped joint is not very difficult, and it will look good even when the corner isn't square.

Butt Joint. (A) The most common use of a butt joint occurs where baseboard meets casing. **(B)** If a butt joint is cut at any angle other than exactly 90 degrees, a gap will show up against the casing.

Miter Joint. (A) In a properly-cut miter joint, all edges and surfaces of the two pieces will intersect precisely at the miter. **(B)** One sign of a poor miter joint is a small gap at the outside of the joint. **(C)** Another sign of a poor miter joint is a misalignment of mating pieces. This sometimes happens when one piece is cut at an angle slightly different from that of the other piece.

3 Installation

Trimming a Miter

Using a Plane. Because many wall corners aren't exactly square, the ends of a miter joint must sometimes be trimmed with a block plane in order to make a perfect fit. When trimming a miter that doesn't fit exactly, remove wood from the back side of the cut until the front edges meet. To avoid chipping the front edges of the molding, trim the molding by removing material from the back side as shown.

Making Off-Angle Cuts. To miter moldings for a non-standard corner, you'll have to bisect the angle. An easy way to do this is to draw layout lines parallel with each wall and about a foot away from them. Then use a sliding T-bevel to copy the angle so that you can transfer it to your power miter saw or miter box.

Miters on Non-Plumb Walls. Unfortunately, not all walls are plumb (vertical). If the corner leans out, the top edge of the wall trim will be tight but a gap will show at the bottom. You might be able to live with this flaw on base trim—moldings at foot level aren't as closely scrutinized as others—but on ceiling trim the flaw will be visually obnoxious. Fix it by cutting a compound miter. Or if an outside miter is open just slightly, you may be able to close it by rubbing the corner with a nail set, which will slightly fold over the outside edge of the miter, making the gap imperceptible.

Using a Power Miter Saw or Miter Box. You can make more accurate fitting adjustments by using a power miter saw or miter box.

■ *Correcting a Corner That Is More Than 90 Degrees.* To bring them together, cut one angle slightly less than 45 degrees, and retry the fit. If it still doesn't fit, recut the other angle in the same way. Repeat the process until you have a tight fit.

■ *Correcting a Corner That Is Less Than 90 Degrees.* Cut the angle a little more than 45 degrees.

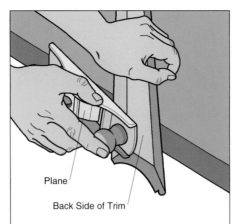

Using a Plane. When trimming a miter that doesn't fit exactly, remove some wood from the back side of the cut until the front edges meet.

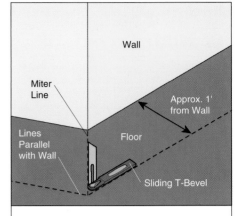

Making Off-Angle Cuts. Draw a line from the corner of the wall to the corner of your layout lines, and use a sliding T-bevel to transfer the angle.

Miters on Non-Plumb Walls. Walls that are out of plumb create special problems when trim must meet at a corner. Unless you make a compound miter cut, the joint will not fit properly. Be sure to start at outside corners, if any, to prevent pieces from being cut too short when adjusting.

MItered Return. When a piece of trim (such as base molding) terminates on a wall without meeting another piece, you can simply crosscut it to length. However, this will expose the end grain of the wood, which is difficult to paint. A neater solution is called a "mitered return" or a "return in itself." The end of the base is mitered, and then a small piece of matching molding is mitered and used to cap the end of the base.

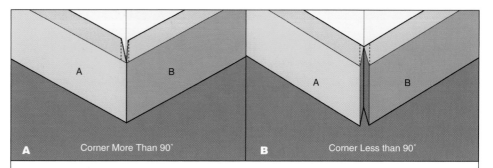

Corner More Than 90° | Corner Less than 90°

Using a Power Miter Saw or Miter Box. (A) To adjust the fit of a base miter, cut angle "A" slightly less than 45 degrees. If the fit still isn't tight, do the same with angle "B." **(B)** To cut an angle of more than 45 degrees on some power miter saws, you may have to place a small shim between the workpiece and the saw fence. The angle of cut will increase depending on the thickness of the shim. Always start with outside corners, if any, to prevent a short measure at other end of piece.

Mitered Return. A return is used to continue the profile of a molding back to the wall.

Cutting a Compound Miter

A compound miter cut combines a miter and bevel cut simultaneously. **(A)** The cut end is 45 degrees to the edge and 30 degrees to the face of the wood, in this case. Only compound miter saws can make this kind of cut without using a jig or shim. Figuring out the specific angles can be tricky. **(B)** Rather than try to figure out all of the angles to make a compound miter cut, simply use a wooden miter box and a shim to make the cut. Shim the top of the miter box so that the base leans against it at the same angle as the wall angle, and then make the miter cut.

Coping Base Trim

Cutting a coped joint is not difficult, but it does call for careful work and a dash of patience. The value of the coped joint, as opposed to a miter, is that it won't as easily show a gap if the trim shrinks slightly.

1 Installing the First Piece. Crosscut the first piece of trim, and butt it into the corner.

2 Making a Miter Cut. Cut a 45-degree miter on the intersecting piece of base trim.

3 Cutting with a Coping Saw. Use a coping saw to cut along the front edge of the miter.

4 Making the 90-Degree Cut. Remove excess trim at the bottom to form a slightly undercut 90-degree angle. Test the fit by slipping the coped piece into place against the first piece of trim.

5 Making Trim Cuts. Use a flat file or utility knife to fine-tune the back side of the cut. Retest the fit until you are happy with it.

6 Installing the Second Piece. The two cuts should produce a face that fits the contours of the piece to which it is butted.

Even base molding with a very simple profile should be coped for the best fit. Note that where the two pieces meet at the top edge, a very fine piece of wood will overlap from the coped piece to the butted piece. Take care during installation not to damage this fragile point. For a tight fit, molding that is coped should be cut a bit long and then "sprung" into place. You'll have to experiment a bit to find out how much spring your molding has, and therefore how much longer to make it. Cut properly, the molding will snap into place with light pressure. If you have to force the molding into place, however, it is too long and will probably push adjacent molding out of position.

1 Butt the first piece of molding tightly into the corner.

2 Pencil a 90° angle on the top of the edge of molding.

3 Angling the saw slightly away from the edge of the miter, cut down to front edge.

4 Remove the remaining 45° angle at the bottom of molding with a miter saw.

5 You may have to remove some wood so the front edge of the cope fits properly.

6 Well-cut contours fit together perfectly.

Making a Scarf Joint

A scarf joint is used to join lengths of trim end to end. Though trim typically comes in lengths long enough to cover a wall in one piece, this won't always be the case, particularly if you're trying to make the most of the trim you have on hand. A scarf joint is made by mitering the ends of two pieces of trim in opposite directions and then overlapping them. When joined, the overlapping pieces combine to make a flush surface. This joint is preferable to a butt joint because it won't show an obvious gap if the wood shrinks slightly in length.

The joint should occur over a wall stud whenever possible. This will allow you to nail through the joint and into the stud for a strong connection. Nails should be driven at an angle so that they fasten both splices to the stud.

1. Cut a 45-degree miter on trim #2, and nail the trim in place. Get an approximate measurement for trim #1; find a piece several inches longer than you need; and then cut a 45-degree miter on one end, as shown. Test-fit the second piece, and crosscut it to final length.

2. Nail through the top of the scarf joint and into a stud. Nail straight so that you can easily make the pieces flush when you countersink the nail.

Cutting Picture Molding

Picture molding is a ceiling molding that's installed somewhat differently from cove molding and crown molding. If the picture molding will actually be used to support heavy pictures (as opposed to serving a purely decorative function), it should be fastened to the wall studs with 2-inch long drywall screws. This will prevent it from pulling loose under the accumulated weight of many pictures. Also unlike crown and cove, picture molding need not be cut upside down. Instead, cut it exactly as it would lie on the wall. Picture molding is generally mitered on both inside and outside corners; it is not usually coped.

Strengthening Joints

Two effective methods of strengthening joints are incorporating wood blocking and biscuits.

Adding Blocking

Even the tightest of joints won't last very long if you don't nail into something solid behind it. If you plan ahead, you can add blocking to a wall as it is being framed. For instance, chair rail can be nailed to 2x4 stock installed between the studs or to 1x4 stock recessed into notches cut into the studs. In either case, make sure the stock is securely face-nailed or toenailed into place to provide a solid nailing surface to which the trim can be attached.

Installing Biscuits

A problem with butt and miter joints is that they can open up as the wood shrinks. One way to eliminate this problem is to join trim with wood splines called "biscuits." Biscuits are football-shaped pieces of compressed wood that fit into a semi-circular cut made by a special tool called a plate joiner. Use white or yellow woodworker's glue to install biscuits; the glue makes the biscuit expand slightly, which makes the joint extra-strong.

Adding Blocking. Add 1x4 or 2x4 stock to the wall as it is being framed to provide additional support for trim. A block at the corner of the wall provides extra nailing surface for the ends of base molding.

1 **Marking the Trim.** Use a pencil to mark the two sides of the cut.

2 **Marking the Slots.** Line up the centerline of the plate joiner with the layout marks on the trim, and make a slot in each side of the joint.

3 **Securing the Joint.** Glue a biscuit into the slots with white or yellow woodworker's glue and bring the joint together.

1 Mark the two sides of the cut.

Fence

Guide Board

2 Make a slot in each side of the joint.

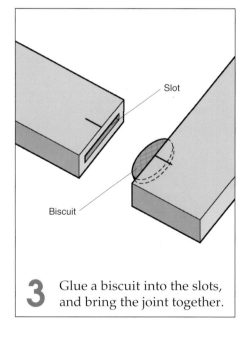

Slot

Biscuit

3 Glue a biscuit into the slots, and bring the joint together.

Finding Studs

If you will be installing trim in an existing home, be ready to spend some time searching for studs. The most reliable method is to use an electronic stud finder. This handheld device, which you can buy at most hardware stores, finds the framing behind the wall surface by measuring changes in the wall's density. You can also use a magnetic stud finder that "homes in" on the nails holding the drywall to the studs.

If you don't have either type of stud finder, you can sink finishing nails into the wall until you hit a stud, or tap along the wall until the hollow sound gives way to the solid sound of a stud. In most houses, subsequent framing members will be spaced every 16 inches (centerline to centerline) from that point. You can also drill a small hole in the wall and probe through it with a stiff wire until you hit a stud. Then hold the wire where it penetrates the wall, pull it out, and use it to measure the

distance to the stud. This usually works only on uninsulated interior walls, however. Another trick is a simple one: by shining a light at raking angles over a wall, you can sometimes see telltale dimples over each nail where the patching compound shrunk. Finally, you can use a makeshift stud finder to find studs by first locating the nails used to secure drywall to them. Slowly pass a magnet over the wall surface; where it "grabs" there's a nail. Locate several nails to verify the location of the stud.

Finding Studs. (A) Using a stud finder is a simple matter of pressing a button and slowly dragging the device across the wall. A series of lights come on to show you the edge and the center of each stud or joist. **(B)** When probing for studs with a nail, work where the resulting nailholes will be covered by the trim you plan to install. **(C)** You can sometimes locate studs by probing through the wall with a stiff wire. **(D)** If you can find the nails used to attach the drywall, you'll know where the studs are. A magnet helps you here.

3 Installation

Installing Ceiling Molding

Like many projects, installing ceiling molding begins with some planning.

The idea is to figure out which joints will be coped, which will be mitered, and which will simply butt to the wall. If your walls are unusually long, you'll have to splice two shorter pieces with a scarf joint. (See "Making a Scarf Joint," page 35.) Your layout plans should note where that joint will go (over which stud, in other words).

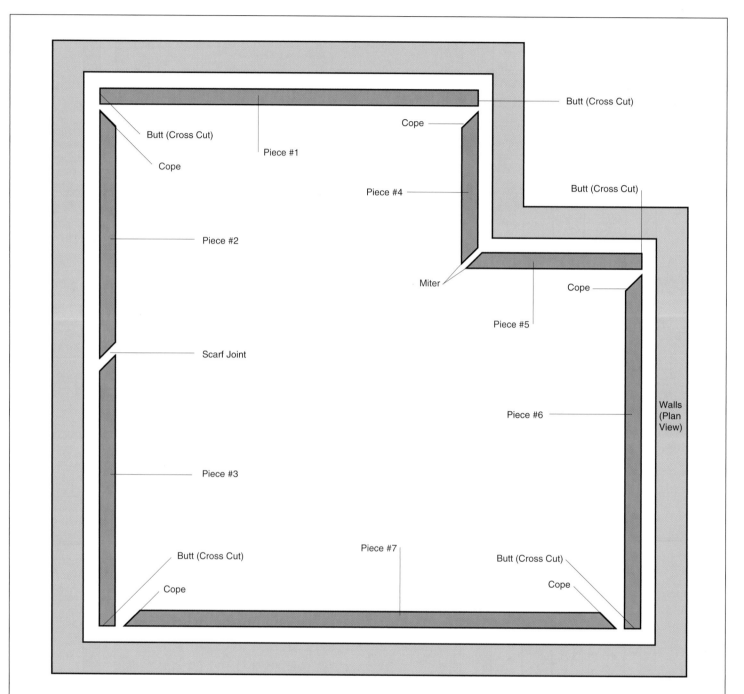

Installing Ceiling Molding. You can start on any wall, but the first piece to be installed will be butted to both opposing walls (piece #1 in this example). Each cope will fit against a butt, and the only place requiring a miter joint is on outside corners.

Measuring for Ceiling Molding

You should also get a rough idea of the lengths of molding you'll need. Measuring for ceiling molding can be difficult to do single-handedly because nobody is there to hold the other end of the measuring tape for you. There are several ways to get around this minor problem, however. The easiest is also the simplest; use a nail to hold one end of the tape. The hole will probably be covered later on by the molding, but if not you can always dab it with a bit of paintable caulk to make it disappear.

Sometimes it's tricky to get an exact measurement between walls, however, because the measuring tape won't fit tightly into a corner. You can use a combination square to give the tape a more accurate "reach," or you can replace the tape altogether with two lengths of straight stock as shown.

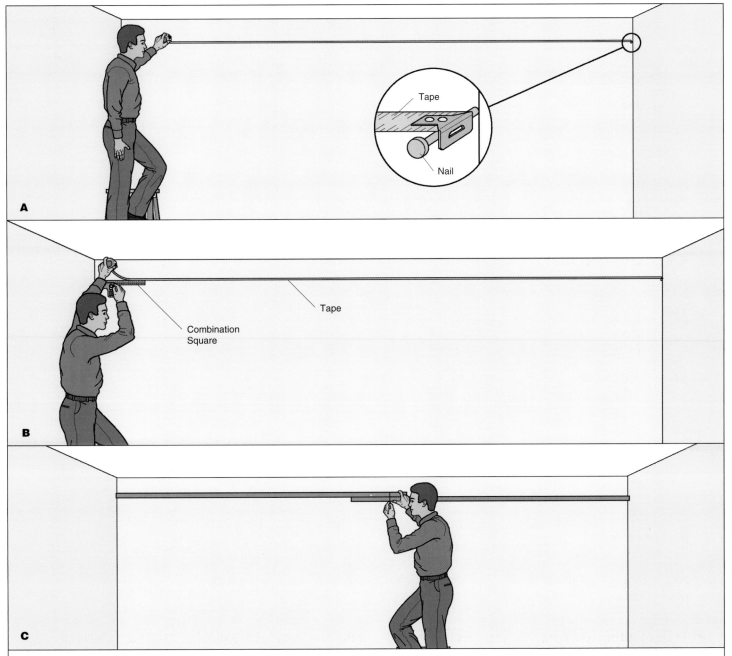

Measuring for Ceiling Molding. (A) Hook the end of a measuring tape on a small nail. Position it to hold the tape's hook close to the wall and ceiling. **(B)** To get an accurate reading in a corner, "extend" it with a combination square. Add the length of the blade to your measurement. **(C)** Measuring sticks can be used when working solo. Slip them to each wall, and make a mark where they overlap. Lay the sticks out on the floor (with marks lined up) and measure the total length with your tape.

Vaulted Ceilings & Molding

Standard ceiling molding won't fit properly where surfaces meet at other than 90 degrees, such as where a vaulted ceiling meets the wall. Use window casing instead.

1 Duplicate the angle between the wall and the ceiling by using a sliding T-bevel as the cutting guide.

2 Use the T-bevel to transfer the angle to the end of the casing, and draw your cut line from the top front corner.

3 You'll get the most accurate cut on the casing using a table saw. You can set up the blade to slightly overcut the angle, as shown in the detail view. This way, the top casing will meet the ceiling exactly.

Drywall

Drywall

1 Use a sliding T-bevel as a cutting guide for molding.

2 Mark correct angle on edge of molding.

3 Molding can be overcut so edge meets ceiling.

When to Install Trim

Whether you're remodeling an older home or building a new one, the installation of trim comes near the end of the project. Exterior trimwork goes on just before the house is painted. Indoor trimwork can be installed anytime after interior wall surfaces are complete and the joints (in the case of drywall) are taped. Be sure that drywall joints are smoothly tapered before you begin to install the trim, otherwise gaps will show behind any trim that crosses a joint, such as ceiling molding and the top edges of base molding and chair rail.

Joint Compound

Trim

Poor Drywall Joint

Drywall

Installing Crown Molding

Crown molding has a reputation for being difficult to install. But while installing crown is a bit more complicated than installing other moldings, it's certainly within reach of most do-it-yourselfers. The joints required are standard ones: butt, cope, and miter. The trick is to take the work a step at a time. The first step is to mark some layout lines on the wall. The method shown accounts for any imperfections in a ceiling that is not perfectly level.

Marking Layout Lines

1 Measuring for Crown Molding. With the tongue and the blade of a framing square representing the wall and the ceiling respectively, hold a piece of crown molding as shown to determine how far below the ceiling its bottom edge will be. Call this distance "A."

2 Drawing a Reference Line. Draw a level reference line on the wall a few inches below this point. A long level is the best tool to use, though you may prefer to snap a chalk line.

3 Finding the Low Point. Measure up to the ceiling at various points in the room to find its low point. Make a mark at distance "A" below this point. Measure up to this mark from your reference line. Do the same around the room's perimeter. Snap a second line at this height.

4 Installing the Molding. Line up the molding's bottom edge with this second line, and nail the top edge directly up into the ceiling joists. Remaining gaps can be filled with drywall compound or paintable caulk.

If the ceiling is greatly out of level, a level molding will highlight the problem and will leave a too-large gap between the top of the molding and the ceiling. In these cases, it's better to install the molding parallel with the ceiling. This will, however, complicate the fitting of joints.

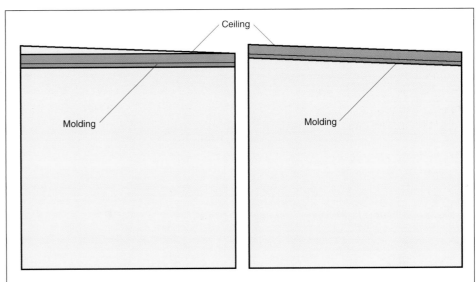

Marking Layout Lines. A level molding can sometimes accentuate the problem of a ceiling that is not level. In such cases, it may be better to let the molding follow the line of the ceiling.

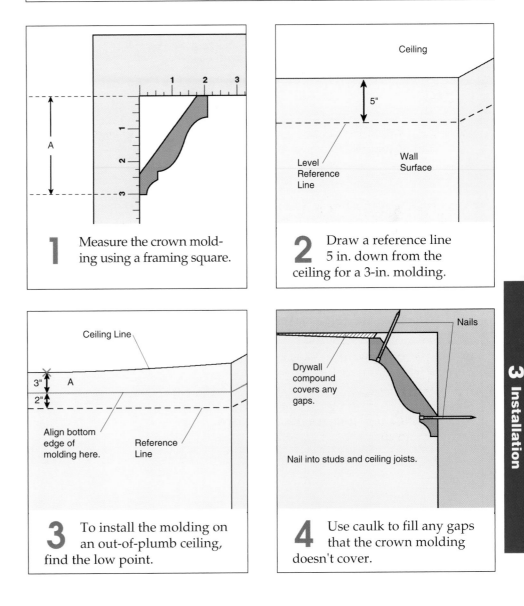

1 Measure the crown molding using a framing square.

2 Draw a reference line 5 in. down from the ceiling for a 3-in. molding.

3 To install the molding on an out-of-plumb ceiling, find the low point.

4 Use caulk to fill any gaps that the crown molding doesn't cover.

Cutting Crown Molding

Though some people find crown molding difficult to install, it's usually not the joinery itself that causes the problems: all that's needed is a 45-degree miter cut and some work with a coping saw. The tricky part is the way you put the molding in a basic miter box for that 45-degree cut. Once you've seen it done, however, cutting crown will no longer seem mysterious. To get the hang of it, make some practice cuts on lengths of scrap crown molding first. Even professionals sometimes find this a useful warmup exercise.

1. Cut and install the adjoining molding. Start by crosscutting a length of crown at both ends so that it fits nicely between opposing walls. Nail it in place.

2. Cut the inside miter joint. When using a basic miter box, place the crown molding upside down. That is, the edge that will go against the ceiling when you install the molding should be placed against the bottom of the miter box when you cut it.

3. Cope the miter. Use a coping saw to cut along the profile line created by the saw. The profile line is the front edge of the molding.

4. Check the fit. Hold the coped piece of molding against the piece installed earlier to check the fit.

Trim the back side of the molding, if necessary, to make a tight fit, using a file or a knife.

5. Cut the other end of the molding. **(A)** If the other end will be part of an inside corner, simply cut it square to fit against the opposite wall; the next piece of crown will be coped to fit it. **(B)** If the other end will be part of an outside corner, place it in the miter box right side up (as it would appear on the wall). Then cut it at 45 degrees. To provide support while cutting the molding, rest its front edge against the saw's fence and hold it securely during the cut.

1. Crown Molding — 90° Cut — 90° Cut

2. Wooden Stop Screwed to Fence — Crown Ready for Cutting — Top Edge at Circle

5. Butt — Coped — Molding — Coped Cut on Next Piece

A.

B. Top (Will Go against Ceiling)

Crown Molding Problems

Cutting crown molding is, in many respects, no different than cutting other profiled moldings. It does, however, present some special problems. For example, if any part of an installed crown molding dips below an imaginary line level, that crown will be impossible to cope. Avoid such profiles, or plan to miter the joints instead of coping them.

Walls parallel with the ceiling joists are often a problem because there's nothing into which you can nail. One solution is to install blocking at the wall-ceiling joint, as shown, and then nail and glue the crown molding to the blocking. Blocking can be made from solid wood or plywood.

When there's no joist or blocking into which to nail, you can put some construction adhesive behind the molding (where it contacts the ceiling). Then toenail it as best you can until the adhesive grips.

Cutting Cove Molding. The procedure for cutting ceiling cove molding is the same as that used for cutting crown. The molding is placed in the miter box with the ceiling edge down so that it can be held firmly in place.

Cutting Cove Molding. Place the molding in the miter box, ceiling edge down.

Crown Molding Problems. (A) This crown molding has a profile that cannot be coped. The portion of the molding below the line level shown here would interfere with the cut. **(B)** This is a typical nailing pattern for crown molding (shown here as a mitered outside corner). If you can't nail into framing at these points and can't provide blocking as an alternative, use construction adhesive to hold the molding against the ceiling. **(C)** Two methods of blocking behind crown molding are solid blocking and two-piece blocking.

Installing Base Trim

Lay out base trim in a manner similar to that for ceiling molding: by arranging the pieces whenever possible so that each has a butt joint on one end and a cope or miter on the other.

Once you get the feel for installing base, the work goes more quickly. Though all trim should be installed with care, there's a bit more allowance for imperfection in base because it is not nearly as visible as other trim. You can measure all the pieces before cutting them, or you can hold each one up against the wall and mark where it should be cut.

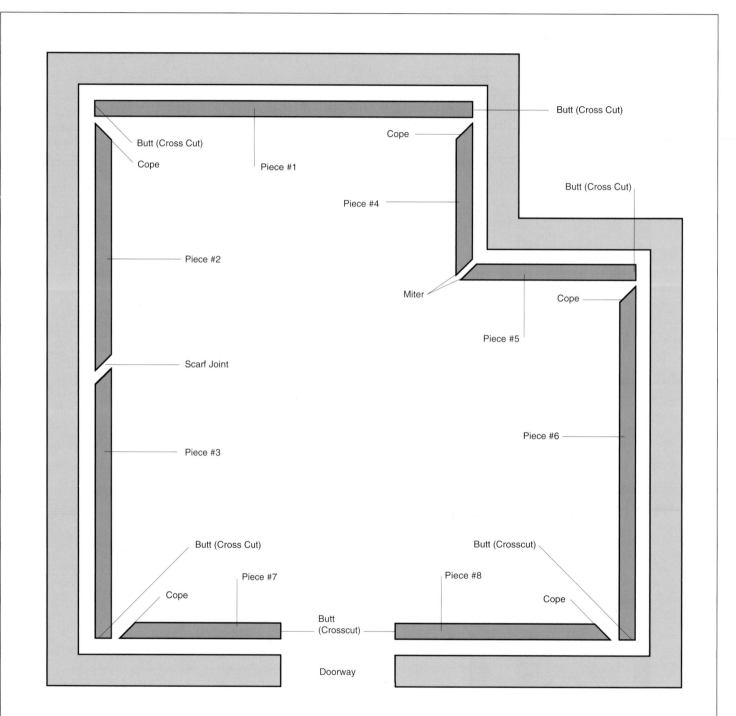

Installing Base Trim. This layout for base trim is similar to the one for crown molding in the same room. The chief difference is that pieces #7 and #8 will butt into the sides of the door casing. Also, it's more acceptable to have a scarf joint in base trim because it is less visible than a scarf joint on ceiling trim such as crown molding.

1 **Cutting the Base Trim.** Cut the base trim to rough lengths, and distribute the pieces around the room.

2 **Mitering the Pieces.** Start with an outside corner, if there is one. Miter and fit the first piece, and then tack it temporarily in place. Cut lengths of base slightly long so that you have to bow them a little to get them into place. This will guarantee tight joints.

3 **Tacking the Base in Place.** Work your way around the room, tacking each length of base in place temporarily. For coped joints, set the nails on the square-cut piece before fitting the coped piece.

4 **Nailing the Base.** After all of the base trim is in place and you're sure the pieces are where you want them, drive all nails home and countersink them using a nail set.

Types of Base

In most homes, every room has at least simple base trim. Base can consist of a single molded piece or a three-part arrangement that consists of a flat section with a base cap on top and a quarter-round shoe along its bottom edge. Profiled base trim must be coped at inside corners. Flat profiles are butted.

Single-piece base is relatively easy to install. Built-up base is more difficult, in part because the base shoe (and sometimes the base cap) is installed after the main portion of the base trim. They are coped or mitered separately.

Base Cap

Flat Trim

Base Shoe

Single-Piece Base

Three-Piece Built-Up Base

1 At this point, the base trim needs only to be cut to the approximate size.

2 Mark the base for the finish cut; make it slightly longer than needed.

3 Use finishing nails to tack the base in place; set nails at coped joints first.

4 Holding the nail set like this makes it easier to drive nails close to the floor.

Installing Base Shoe Molding

When a floor is uneven, base trim may have gaps beneath it in places. A shoe molding is meant to cover these gaps. Because it is slender, it can more easily follow the contours of the floor. Another common use of shoe molding is to cover the edges of newly installed sheet vinyl flooring.

■ Be sure to nail into the base, not the floor.

■ Use the shoe molding to cover slight gaps between the base trim and flooring.

Fitting Base Trim to Vertical Trim

Where base pieces meet door casings or other vertical trim, you'll have to make accurate butt joints. Though the joint itself is simple, its location near the most traveled part of any room makes it a visible joint. One way to ensure accuracy is to mark the cuts using a homemade marking gauge made from ½-inch plywood. The gauge is notched to fit around the base. Hold it firmly to the edge of the vertical trim, and draw a line on the face of the base using the gauge as a guide.

Making a Half-Lap

Some types of base, particularly those with simple profiles that are fully rounded at the top, are difficult to cope and awkward to handle because the top edge of the coped piece will be thin and fragile. One solution is to butt the flat part of the base and miter the curved part. This is called a half-lap miter.

A half-lap miter joint is a combination of several cuts; a miter, a cope, and a butt joint. The joint is time consuming to make but makes a particularly fine finishing touch on moldings with a full, rounded-over top.

1 Mitering the First Piece. First, use a handsaw and miter box to cut a miter in piece #1; in depth, the cut should stop where the base

Installing Base Shoe Molding. (A) Fasten the shoe with 4d nails, driving them into the base trim, not into the floor. **(B)** The base need not be removed when installing vinyl flooring. Base shoe covers what would be a dirt-catching gap between the flooring and the base.

Fitting Base Trim to Vertical Trim. Slip a marking gauge over the base to mark the base cutting locations.

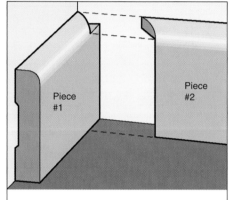

Making a Half-Lap. The half-lap miter is assembled using 8d nails.

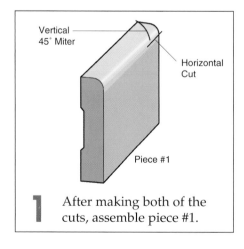

1 After making both of the cuts, assemble piece #1.

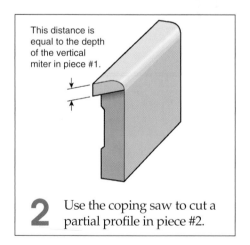

2 Use the coping saw to cut a partial profile in piece #2.

stops curving. Finish it off with a horizontal cut.

2 Mitering and Coping the Second Piece. Then cut a full 45-degree miter on the end of piece

#2, just as you would in preparation for a standard cope. But instead of cutting the entire profile away with a coping saw, cut away only part of it.

Installing Wall Trim

Wall and base trim are relatively common, but wall trim is less so. This makes it all the more effective when thoughtfully designed and installed properly. Each installation has its own peculiarities.

Chair Rail. As with ceiling and base trim, lay out chair rail with the outside corners mitered and the inside corners butted and coped. Apart from its functional value in protecting the walls, chair rail is ideal for dividing the wall into sections that can be given separate decorative treatments. For example, you can wallpaper the lower portion of a wall, then cover the exposed top edges of the paper with chair rail. If you also plan to add base trim after the papering, you won't have to be too precise about the bottom edges of the paper.

Wainscoting. Wainscoting is generally a decorative or protective wood facing that is applied to the lower portion of an interior wall, though other treatments such as tile, wallpaper, or even paint can be used. Wainscoting can be as complicated as you wish to make it. There is no standard height, though the top of wainscoting is usually the same height as chair rail, which is 32 to 36 inches from the floor.

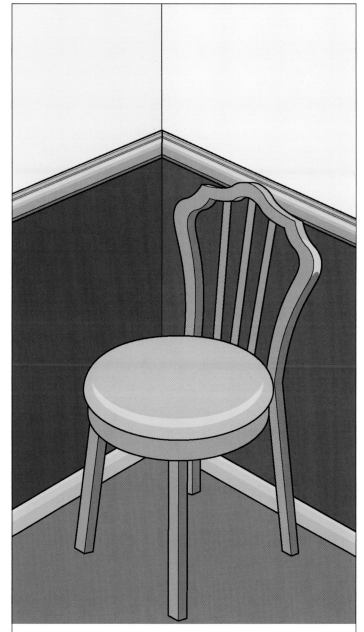

Chair Rail. You would typically put the height of a chair rail at 32 to 36 in. from the floor.

Wainscoting. Using wainscoting on a staircase offers protection against handprints.

Installing Wainscoting

A simple way to apply wainscoting is to use tongue-and-groove boards capped with molding. They are available in a variety of woods, depending on regional preferences, but most often they are some type of softwood. The interlocking nature of the boards makes spacing them fairly easy. One alternative to installing wainscoting of individual boards is to use plywood paneling.

1 Marking Layout Lines. Mark a level reference line on the wall for the top of the wainscot. Measure the width of the area to determine how many pieces you'll need. You may have to rip the first and last panels to width.

2 Cutting the Boards. Cut the wainscot boards slightly less than the distance from the floor to the reference line. This will accommodate any variations in the floor.

3 Laying Out the Wall. Lay out the boards on the wall. Rip the end pieces to the same width.

4 Nailing the Boards. Nail the boards in place one by one, holding each against the layout line. Periodically, check the edges of the boards with a level; straighten any that are getting out of plumb.

5 Applying Base Cap. Cover the top of the wainscot with base caps or other trim, and finish off the bottom with base.

1 Draw the reference line at the desired wainscot height.

2 Cut the boards slightly short, leaving a ¼-in. gap at bottom.

3 Rip the first and last board to the proper width, as indicated by the dashed cutting line.

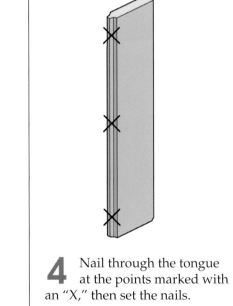

4 Nail through the tongue at the points marked with an "X," then set the nails.

5 Use one of the base caps shown above, or you can design and make your own.

Other Molding

Screen Molding. Screen molding is a half-round or flat profiled molding that's used to protect the cut edges of an insect screen that has been nailed to a wooden frame. Leave the screen a bit long on all sides. After the molding is in place, use a utility knife to trim the screen flush with the molding.

Shelf Face Edging. The edges of plywood or particleboard shelves are usually dressed with some type of trim, whether a half-round or profiled molding or a simple piece of finish wood. For ¾-inch-thick shelves, nail the facings with 4d nails. For extra strength, add a bead of glue to the back of the molding before nailing.

Corner Molding. Used to dress and protect the outside corners of a paneled wall, corner molding can also be added to drywall corners. It's usually cut with a butt joint on each end to fill the vertical space between base and ceiling trim.

Screen Molding. This type of screen molding is mitered at all four corners and fastened to the screen frame with wire brads.

Shelf Face Edging. Edging covers the exposed edge grain of the shelving and stiffens it.

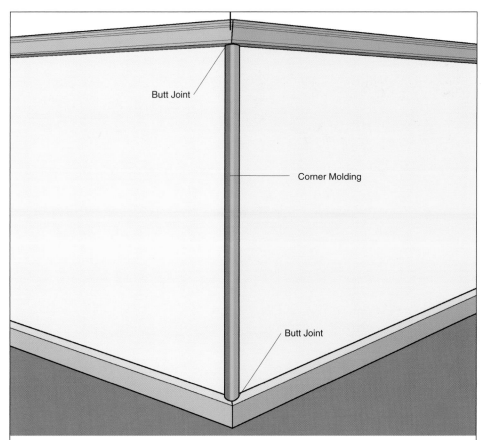

Corner Molding. If corner molding runs between ceiling and base trim, it must be thinner than both types of trim in order to look right. If the base has a molded top edge, it will be difficult to make the corner molding fit properly.

Solving Common Problems

Trim is often used to conceal joints inside and outside a house. Indoors, these joints can be found wherever a material changes direction (such as where paneling turns a corner) or where natural wood movement would otherwise create unsightly gaps. Outdoors, trim is often more than just cosmetic. Without it, the many joints between surfaces and materials would be subject to water infiltration. The resulting leaks are a nuisance, but even more importantly, wood that gets wet repeatedly encourages wood-destroying insects and fungi to attack it. You probably won't be able to see the results of an infestation until considerable damage has been done.

Interior Trim Solutions

Paneling joints are covered by a variety of trim pieces. If the paneling is prefinished, you can obtain prefinished trim and colored nails to match. Plastic trim is also available to cover the joints of thin sheet paneling.

Astragals are used to prevent one door from swinging past its mate and to help alignment. Weatherstripping can be applied along the inside of the astragal to seal the doors against drafts.

Cove or scotia molding is often used beneath treads, with mitered returns where the side of the tread is exposed to a room. Trim may also be found along the top of the stair stringers to conceal the gap between stringers and treads. In the case of open stairs, such as these, molding is used along the underside of the tread, too.

Though this step is often skipped, all exterior trim-work should be primed to keep the wood from cupping. This includes the back sides and particularly cut edges.

The structural core of exterior posts, such as those supporting the roof of a porch, should be protected from the elements. This 2x4 post is enclosed with trim and detailed with molding; the base conceals flashing. Use hot-dipped galvanized nails.

Trim at the intersection of walls and roof has several purposes. The frieze board prevents windblown rain from getting behind the siding. Bed molding keeps insects from finding their way into the attic.

Trim pieces assembled into cornerboards fit over the sheathing and provide a surface against which to butt the siding (top inset). If trim must be pieced together vertically, cut each board at an angle and install them so that the joint sheds water (bottom inset).

3 Installation

The curved profile of some window casing makes it difficult to mount shade or curtain hardware; **(A)** back-band molding nailed to the casing creates a flat surface wide enough to support the hardware. **(B)** Chair rail may be thicker than the door casing, resulting in an awkward joint where they meet. Instead of replacing the casing, build up its thickness and width with back band.

When adding solid wood (usually ¾ in. thick) paneling to a room that has baseboard heating units, cut the paneling short to clear the heater and trim the opening with corner guard molding. Be sure to maintain appropriate clearances around the heater. (Check with the manufacturer if in doubt.)

In contrast to standard face-frame cabinets, upper cabinets made with European-style cases must be spaced down from the soffit in order to provide backing for the trim. Blocking can be attached directly to the tops of the cabinets; then the trim can be nailed to the blocking.

Decorative plates can be displayed safely using a plate rail. Nail the top and back together, and then add cove molding and shelf bead. Screw the assembly through the wall finish and into the studs; then add crown molding to conceal the screws.

(A) The traditional way to support closet shelving is with a 1x3 shelf cleat nailed into the studs. **(B)** Molding called shelf strip is sometimes available. It looks nicer than a cleat but takes more time to install because corners must be mitered.

openings

Common Joinery for Window & Door Trim

The wood trim around windows and doors is called casing, and it can be installed in all sorts of ways to accentuate a particular decorative style. Generally, the style of the trim (and the joinery used to install it) will be consistent throughout a house. There's no reason, however, not to explore variations on whatever style you choose. In a study, for example, you might want to make the casing more ornate in order to complement other woodwork in the room. In a laundry room, however, you might opt for the simplest casing to save money for more visible rooms.

Nearly all casing installations, however, will use some version of two joints: the miter and the butt. You will never need to cut a coped joint on casing.

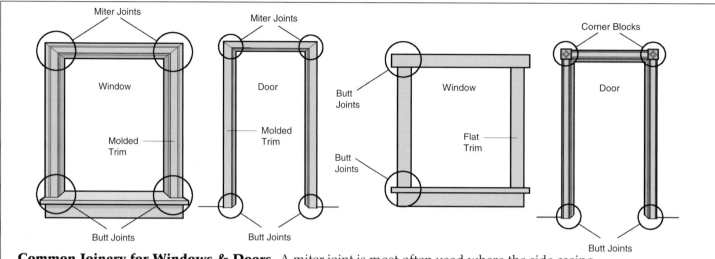

Common Joinery for Windows & Doors. A miter joint is most often used where the side casing joins the head casing. At the sill (on windows) or at the floor (on doors), a butt joint is most common.

Casing Styles

If you walk into different houses around the country, you will probably find mitered casing around the windows and doors (at least indoors; see page 69 for exterior details). This is partly due to economy; this type of casing joinery goes up relatively quickly and is a part of every carpenter's skills. You can, however, use many other styles. In fact, one of the hallmarks of traditional detailing is the extra care and effort spent upon it.

The casing of a door generally follows the style of any window casing in the same room. When designing the trim detailing for any room, therefore, make sure that you consider casing that will look good both on windows and on doors. Sometimes windows can look a little overwhelmed by the same casing that looks terrific on a door.

Flat Head Casing (Overhangs Slightly) Corner Blocks with Molded Casing Mitered Casing

Wall Problems

Casing is nailed to the window jamb or doorjamb and to the wall. In order for the casing to fit properly, however, the edges of the jamb must be in the same plane as the wall surface. In other words, they must be "flush." Any difference between them will show up as a gap.

Testing the Surface. Before installing the casing, place a straightedge over the edges of the jambs and wall surface. You can usually see a difference that you wouldn't notice otherwise.

Filling the Gap. If the difference between them is less than ⅛ inch, any gap that shows up around the casing can most likely be concealed with paintable caulk. This isn't an option, however, if the casing and jambs are to be stained instead of painted.

Shaving a High Wall. If the wall is slightly "higher" than the jamb, you can shave it down with a shaping tool. You may want to draw guidelines on the drywall to ensure that you don't remove more than will be covered by the casing.

Trimming the Jamb. If the jamb is higher than the wall, shave it down with a block plane. If you notice the problem before installing the door or window, you may be able to cut down the jambs using a circular saw.

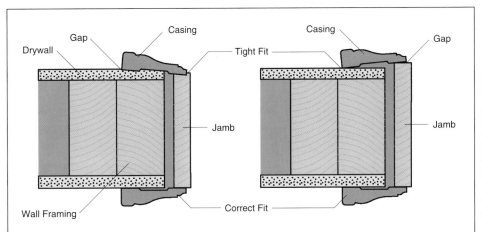

Wall Problems. If the wall surface is not flush with the jamb, you will have a gap at one side of the casing.

Testing the Surface. Hold a straightedge against the jambs and wall surface to detect any gaps.

Filling the Gap. Use paintable latex caulk to fill gaps less than ⅛ in.

Shaving a High Wall. Remove small amounts of drywall using a shaping tool; coarse-grit sandpaper will also work. Be careful not to damage the surrounding wall surfaces.

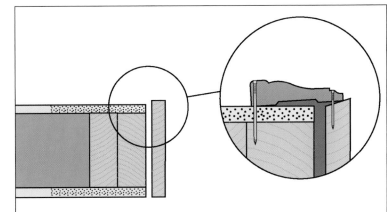

Trimming a Jamb. If you're shaving down the jamb with a plane, bevel it slightly toward the wall to prevent a gap (inset). Nail only at the outer edge of the casing, nailing in the middle will crack it.

Jamb Extensions

In some cases, the edges of the jamb will fall short of the surrounding wall surface by a considerable amount, and no amount of planing or filing will bring them together. This may be true if your walls are unusually thick. Custom windows can be built to fit the thickness of these walls, but this is very expensive. A more economical approach is to buy windows and doors with conventional-size jambs and then fit them with jamb extensions.

Jamb extensions are wood strips nailed to the inside edges of the jambs to make up the difference between the jamb width and wall thickness. When ordering windows, order the jamb extensions at the same time, or make your own using a table saw. If you're planning to stain or use a clear finish on the jambs and trim, the jamb extensions should be made of the same wood as the windows. If you're painting everything, be sure to use an inexpensive and easy-to-work lumber, such as pine, for the extensions. Just be sure that whatever wood you use is straight and relatively clear. Because jamb extensions are so slender, any knots will make them too fragile to work with.

1 Making Jamb Extensions.
Jamb extensions are added after the installation of the window, and are easily made on a table saw. Using this saw with a rip fence will ensure that the extensions are cut uniform.

Caution: *Whenever cutting wood into thin strips, use a push stick or some other method to keep fingers well away from the saw blade.*

2 Installing Jamb Extensions.
Jamb extensions are sometimes installed so that the inner face is flush with the surface of the jamb, but they can also be offset slightly. If you offset the extensions, round off the sharp edges of the jamb before installing them; paint holds better to slightly rounded edges. Use finishing nails long enough to penetrate at least 1 inch into the jamb.

1 Jamb extensions can be cut as needed from a wider board. By drawing a pencil line across the best faces of the cut jamb extensions, you will install them properly.

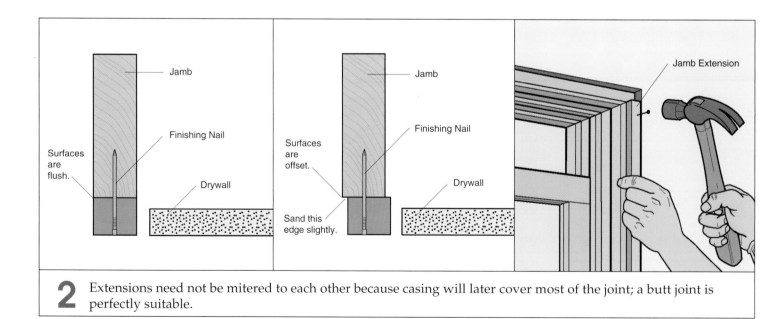

2 Extensions need not be mitered to each other because casing will later cover most of the joint; a butt joint is perfectly suitable.

Installing the Stool

Rabbeted stools have an angled underside that matches angled rough sills, while flat stools match flat sills. In either case, installation is the same.

Installing the Stool. The window stool sits against the window sash and on the sill. Stools may be rabbeted or flat to match the sill.

1 Cutting the Stool. First, cut the stool to length. Usually, the "horn" of the stool extends slightly beyond the casing by ½ to 1 inch, but this is primarily an aesthetic decision for you to make. Mark the center of the stool, and make a matching mark on the center of the window frame.

Now hold the stool against the window jambs and align the two center marks. To lay out the horns, slide a combination square along the front edge of the stool until the blade rests against one side jamb of the window, and mark the stool as shown. Repeat this on the other side of the stool.

2 Trimming the Stool. While holding the stool against the casing, measure from its inside edge to the sash. Transfer this measurement (minus $1/16$ inch) to the marks just made in the previous step, and then draw a perpendicular line from each point to the end of the stool. Cut the stool along the layout lines, using a handsaw or a saber saw. The stool should now fit into place on the window.

3 Nailing the Stool. Round over the edges of the stool with sandpaper before installing it—don't forget to round the ends of the horns, too. Nail the stool into the window framing, and set the nails. If the horn of the stool is slender, you can nail through its front edge and into the wall to strengthen it.

1 Square across each stool's end and draw a line from the inside face of the jamb.

2 Measure from the stool to the sash (distance "A"), and then mark out this distance along the line drawn in the previous step. Cut the stool and remove the X portion.

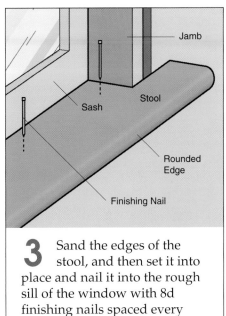

3 Sand the edges of the stool, and then set it into place and nail it into the rough sill of the window with 8d finishing nails spaced every 10 in. or so.

Trimming a Window

"Trimming out" the window is the last step before painting it. This process calls for installing the stool, apron, and casing (generally in that order). In order for each element to be installed correctly, the previous element must be in the right place.

Installing the Apron

The apron is the simplest part of the window trim to install, but even here there's room for a bit of creativity. Decide how long to make the apron and how to deal with its cut ends. Both decisions are a matter of personal taste.

1 **Cutting the Ends.** Some people prefer the ends of the apron to line up with the outside of the casing, while others would rather the ends fall just outside the casing. The difference amounts to fractions of an inch but can have a significant visual impact.

2 **Finishing the Ends.** The ends of the apron can simply be cut square and sanded smooth or finished off professionally. Again, it is a matter of personal preference. Experiment with different combinations to see which you like best.

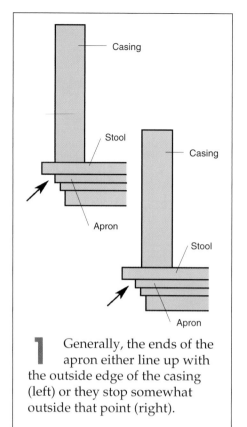

1 Generally, the ends of the apron either line up with the outside edge of the casing (left) or they stop somewhat outside that point (right).

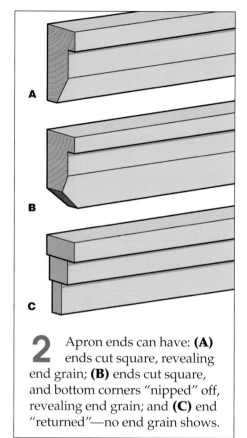

2 Apron ends can have: **(A)** ends cut square, revealing end grain; **(B)** ends cut square, and bottom corners "nipped" off, revealing end grain; and **(C)** end "returned"—no end grain shows.

Cutting a Returned Apron

Of the methods above, cutting a returned apron is the most time consuming, but trim carpenters consider it the mark of a first quality job; many others just think it looks the best. This is because the profile on the face of the apron will turn the corner and "return" to meet the wall surface. No end grain is exposed; the ends of the apron are as smooth as its face. The drawings

below show how to make a return. Note that these steps must be repeated for both ends of the apron.

1. Cut a 45-degree miter lengthwise through one end of the apron.

2. Cut a mating 45-degree miter in the end of a scrap piece of apron.

3. Place the scrap piece face down on the miter saw, and cut off the end just

mitered. This will sever a small, triangular piece of the apron; set it aside for a moment.

4. Nail the apron in place beneath the window stool, and glue the small return created in step 3 into place at the end of the apron. Drill pilot holes, and then secure the return with small brads.

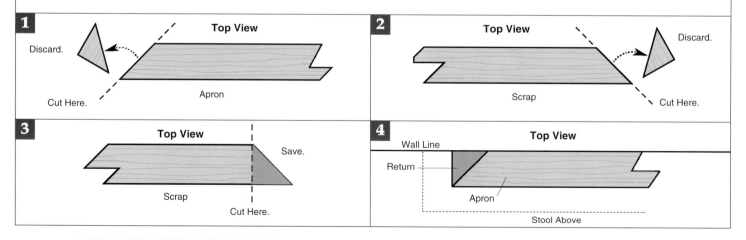

Installing Mitered Casing

Installing window casing is the fussiest part of trimming out a window—any imperfections in the joints will be readily apparent to anyone who cares to look. Though it may take a good bit of patience, especially the first time out, casing a window is not difficult.

1 **Marking the Reveals.** After you have checked to be sure that the edges of the jamb are flush with the wall, mark out reveals on the edges of the jambs, particularly at the corners. A reveal is a slight off-set between the inside face of the jamb and the inside edge of the casing. It's easier to install the casings when not trying to make them perfectly flush with the inside of the jamb, and the small shadow line that results is visually pleasing. To mark the reveals, adjust the blade of a combination square to the size of the reveal and mark the jambs at each corner and at several places along their length. Some carpenters prefer to use a reveal gauge as a guide while tacking the casing in place. (See "Making & Using a Reveal Gauge," page 65.)

2 **Marking the Head Casing.** Hold a length of casing against the reveal lines on the head jamb, and mark the base of each miter. Draw a light slash mark on each end of the casing to identify the direction of the miter. (This will prevent you from cutting it the wrong way when you take your stock to the saw.)

3 **Cutting the Head Casing.** Cut a 45-degree miter on each end of the head casing. The best technique for making any miter cut is to follow the layout mark, leaving just a trace of the pencil mark showing. Tack the casing in place as you line it up with the reveal marks.

1 Mark the reveals along the edges of the window jambs. The reveal should be about ⅛ to 3⁄16 in. wide.

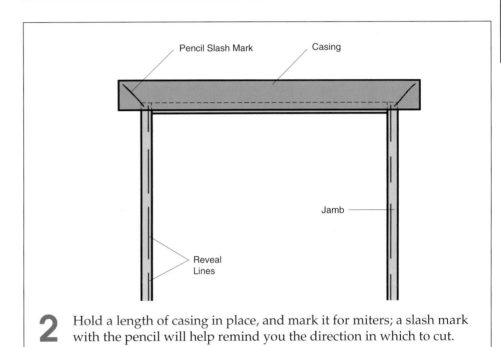

2 Hold a length of casing in place, and mark it for miters; a slash mark with the pencil will help remind you the direction in which to cut.

3 Make a miter cut on each end of the head casing.

Nail

Head
Casing

Jamb

Measure to top
edge of stool.

Measuring Tape

4 Don't assume that both side casings will be exactly the same length. Measure, cut, and fit each side independently.

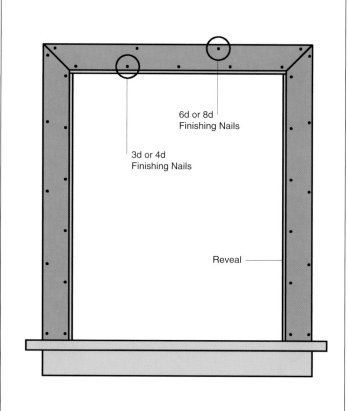

6d or 8d
Finishing Nails

3d or 4d
Finishing Nails

Reveal

5 Nails in the jamb go through the thinnest part of the casing, so they can be small; nails going into the wall must be longer.

4 Marking the Side Casing.
Each side casing will have a miter at one end and a square cut at the other. Make the miter cut first. Then measure from the tip of the head casing to the stool, and transfer this measurement to your stock to provide a cut line for the square cut.

5 Cutting and Fitting the Side Casing. When you make the square cut, make it slightly long—this will allow you some leeway for making a precise fit. Test-fit the casing: line it up against the reveal lines, and cut a sliver off the bottom, if necessary. Tack the casing in place, and repeat the procedure on the second piece of side casing. Adjust head or side casings as needed to get the proper fit all around, and then drive home all of

Predrill holes and
cross-nail here.

6 To strengthen the corners, predrill holes and cross-nail as shown.

the nails. Set them below the surface using a nail set. If you have casing to install on other windows, wait to fill the nailholes until all the casing is done.

6 Strengthening the Corners.
Drill pilot holes through the head and side casings, and drive a 4d finishing nail through each hole.

Adjusting a Miter

In an ideal world, each miter you make would fit exactly the first time. But cuts aren't always perfect, walls aren't always plumb and straight, and jambs aren't always square. When you encounter these situations, your miters won't fit properly unless you adjust them to account for less than ideal conditions.

Wedging when Recutting. You can change the angle of the saw to recut a miter, but it's quicker to wedge the casing away from the saw fence.

Wedging the Miter's Base. A wedge can be positioned to close a gap at the base of the miter.

Wedging the Miter's Tip. If the gap is at the tip of the miter, the wedge must be positioned differently.

Wedging Behind the Miter. If the miters aren't properly aligned after you recut them, a slender wedge behind the miter will probably even them up.

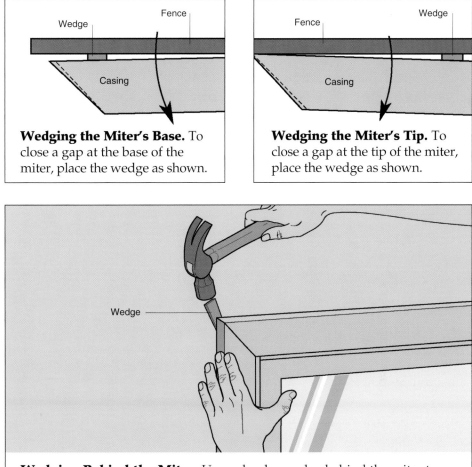

Wedging the Miter's Base. To close a gap at the base of the miter, place the wedge as shown.

Wedging the Miter's Tip. To close a gap at the tip of the miter, place the wedge as shown.

Wedging Behind the Miter. Use a slender wedge behind the miter to achieve proper alignment.

Wedging when Recutting. Be sure that the casing is tight against the wedge and is against the fence in one other place to avoid movement of the casing.

Installing Butt-Jointed Casing

Mitered casing is widespread, but it is hardly universal. Several traditional trim styles rely on an assembly of casing members that entirely eliminate the need for miters. These styles go by various names, but the basic types can be described as built-up casing or corner block casing. Either type can be used on interior doors and windows. Installation calls for laying out the same reveals noted earlier and marking them on the jambs.

Built-Up Casing

Of the two types of butt-jointed casing, the built-up type is the easiest for novices to install. In fact, many find it easier to install than mitered casing because the assembly is more forgiving of minor mistakes in measuring. The casing is usually made from ¾-inch-thick trim stock.

1 **Installing Side Casings.**
Mark out the reveals on the head jamb and side jambs, just as you would for mitered casing. Then hold a length of casing against one side jamb, and mark it at the reveal on the head jamb. (You could measure the distance, but this method is easier and more accurate.) Make a 90-degree cut on the casing at this mark, and then nail the casing in place. Repeat the procedure with the opposite side casing.

2 **Installing the Head Casing.**
The first piece of a two-piece head casing is the same thickness as the side casing but narrower. If the casing is ¾ inch thick, then this first piece can be ⅞ to 1 inch wide, though the exact width is mostly a matter of personal preference. Round over its edges with sandpaper or a router. The second piece of head casing can be nailed to the wall above the first piece.

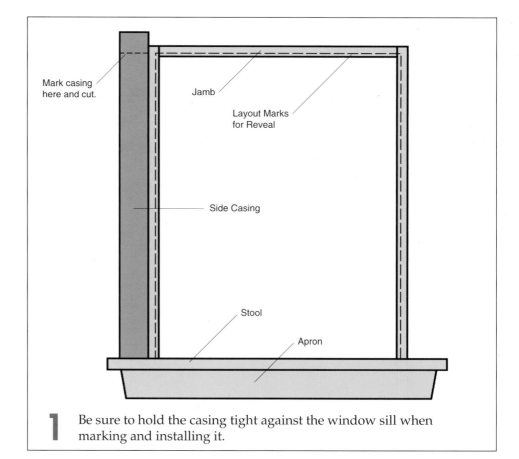

1 Be sure to hold the casing tight against the window sill when marking and installing it.

2 The two-piece head casing can be installed in various combinations. In any case, the edges of the piece installed edgewise should be rounded over with sandpaper or a router.

Corner Block Casing

Many Victorian-style houses feature wood corner blocks at the intersections of head casing with the side casings. The decorative blocks can be made on site but are also available from mail-order suppliers and well-stocked home centers or lumberyards. Head and side casings fit against the corner blocks in a butt joint, rather than meeting in a miter joint. The blocks should be slightly thicker than the casing to conceal the end grain of the casing.

1 Installing the Side Casing.
Mark out the reveals on the head jamb and side jambs. Then hold a length of casing against one side jamb, and mark it at the bottom of the head jamb. Make a 90-degree cut on the casing at this mark, and then nail the casing in place. Repeat the procedure with the opposite side casing.

2 Installing the Corner Blocks.
Each corner block should sit squarely atop the side casing, with its inside corner flush with the corner of the jamb. Predrill two nailholes in each block, and nail it in place. (Predrilling minimizes the chance of splitting the block as you nail it up.)

3 Installing Head Casing.
Measure between the two corner blocks, and cut a piece of casing stock slightly longer (no more than 1/16 inch). Fit the head casing in place, and trim it if necessary for a snug fit. The fit shouldn't be so tight, however, that it pushes the blocks out of position.

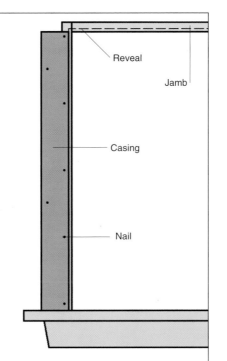

Reveal · Jamb · Casing · Nail

1 Tack the side casing in place; don't drive the nails home until you are satisfied with the position of the corner blocks. This will allow you some leeway for fitting the blocks properly, if necessary.

Corner Block · Jamb · Predrill and Nail · Overhang Here Same as Reveal · Reveal

2 The overhang on the outer edges of the corner blocks is usually about the same as the reveal you marked earlier on the jamb, but this is purely a matter of personal preference.

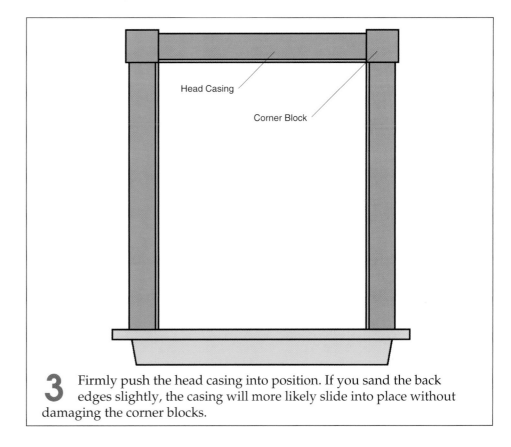

Head Casing · Corner Block

3 Firmly push the head casing into position. If you sand the back edges slightly, the casing will more likely slide into place without damaging the corner blocks.

Installing Picture-Frame Window Casing

Not every window has a stool and an apron. This is sometimes the case with windows that are very high on the wall or with windows in hallways where the projection of a stool would reduce clearances in the halls. Bay and bow windows are often installed without a stool, too. A lower portion of casing (opposite the head casing) is installed to cover the gap between jamb and wall. This style is called picture-frame casing.

Installing picture-frame casing calls for the same skills required for standard casing, though you'll have to mark reveals on all four jambs instead of just on three. The casing can be installed piece by piece, much as you would install standard window casing. An easier way, however, is to cut and assemble the entire "frame" and then install it on the jambs. The jamb corners must be square; check them with a framing square.

Installing Picture-Frame Window Casing. This picture window has casing where the stool and apron would normally be.

1 **Cutting the Miters.** Lay out the reveals, measuring between them to get the casing measurements, and cut all four pieces with a 45-degree miter on each end. Then assemble the "picture frame" face down on a flat surface.

2 **Positioning the Casing.** With all four corners stapled (two in each joint), gently turn the frame over and position it on the window.

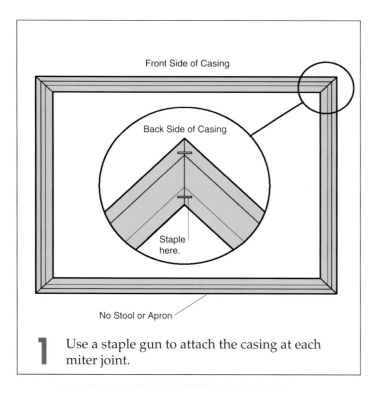

Front Side of Casing

Back Side of Casing

Staple here.

No Stool or Apron

1 Use a staple gun to attach the casing at each miter joint.

2 Adjust the frame's position to correspond to the reveal marks, and nail it into place.

Trimming a Door

Once you've had some experience installing the various trim pieces needed for a window, trimming a door will be easy. A door requires the same measuring process, the same reveals, the same miters, and the same nailing sequence. (See "Installing Mitered Casing," page 59.) If your window frames required jamb extensions, your exterior door's frames probably will, too. But there's no stool to install and no apron. And instead of measuring the side casing to a stool, you measure to the floor.

Note that doors (and sometimes windows) are cased before any other trim elements are installed. This is because base and chair rails will butt into the casing. The casing often serves, in effect, as a termination point for other trim.

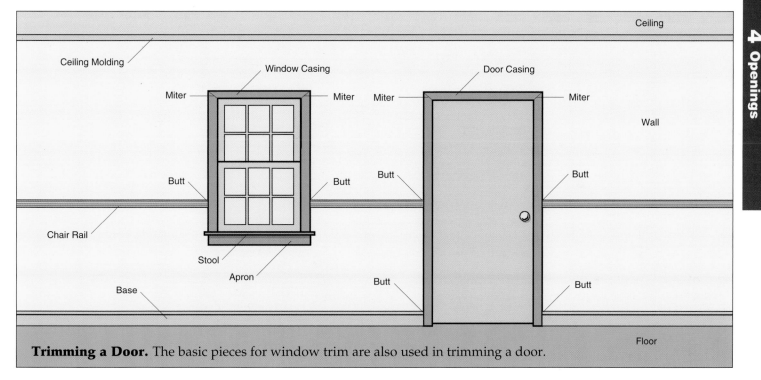

Trimming a Door. The basic pieces for window trim are also used in trimming a door.

Making & Using a Reveal Gauge

Though many people use a combination square to mark out the reveals on doors and windows, a faster way is to use a homemade reveal gauge. The gauge is simply a square of scrap stock with a smaller square screwed to it; the lip formed between the two is exactly the width of the reveal. Using the guide is quicker than using a combination square to lay out the reveals, and will work on any doorjamb or window jamb.

1. Start with a scrap of wood that is perfectly square, and use a combination square to lay out the reveals on one face. Then cut a square smaller on each side by the size of the reveal. Line up two of the edges of the small square exactly along the layout lines on the large square, and then screw the two pieces together.

2. To use the gauge, hold it against the jamb and mark out the reveals or butt casing against it before tacking the trim.

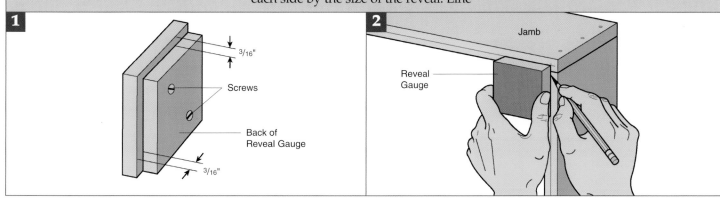

Plumbing Doorjambs

It is particularly important to ensure that the jambs of doors are straight and plumb. This is because the greater length of the side doorjambs will accentuate any imperfection. Also, door casing is probably the most noticeable trim in a house because everyone walks within inches of it, and at least part of the casing is always at eye level.

A properly installed doorjamb should feature side jambs that are plumb and straight, as well as a head jamb that is level. The best way to check the side jambs is with a 4-foot level. (You can also use a plumb bob.) Hold the level against each jamb and check the plumb vial; if the bubble is centered, the jamb is plumb. However, a plumb jamb isn't necessarily straight, so look for any gaps between the level and the jamb as you hold it in place. If you don't have a long level, use a smaller one and hold it against a long, straight board to extend its reach.

Plumbing Doorjambs. You can adjust the doorjamb inward by driving pairs of wedge-shaped shims between the jamb and the framing; to adjust the jamb outward, pull the shims out a bit.

Installing Mitered Door Trim

There are several ways to join head casing to side casing around a door. The most common method is to use a miter joint, which is simply two 45-degree angles joined to make a 90-degree angle. You can use other joints, however, depending on your skill and the architectural style of your house.

1 **Marking the Reveal.** The inside edge of the casing should be offset from the inside edge of the jambs by approximately ⅛ to ³⁄₁₆ inch. The small edge caused by offsetting the two is called a reveal. Set the combination square for the reveal you want, and use it to guide your pencil around the jamb, leaving a line that is ⅛ to ³⁄₁₆ inch from the edge.

2 **Making the First Miter.** Cut a length of casing square at one end. Then place the casing against the reveal line, with the square cut against the floor. Mark the casing at the point where the vertical and horizontal reveal lines intersect, and cut a 45-degree angle at this point.

3 **Making the Next Miters.** Nail the first piece of casing to the jamb with 3d or 4d casing nails spaced every 12 inches or so. Now cut a 45-degree angle on another piece of casing, fit it against the side casing, mark it for the opposite 45-degree angle, and then cut and install it.

4 **Completing the Final Miters.** After installing the head casing, mark, cut, and install the final length of side casing.

5 **Setting the Nails.** After nailing the casing in place, set all of the nails just below the surface of the wood, and then fill the holes with wood putty and sand them smooth when it's dry. Use a nail set and a lightweight hammer to set the nails.

1 Use a combination square to mark the ⅛- to ³⁄₁₆-in. reveal on the jambs.

Reveal Lines

2 Miter where the side casing reveal intersects the head casing reveal.

3 Mark and cut the head casing.

4 Mark and cut the second side casing.

5 Set all nails below the surface of the casing with a nail set and a hammer.

Nail

Surface of Trim

Nail Set

Installing Plinth Blocks

One detail found on some doors that is not found on windows is the plinth block. These decorative blocks provide a transition between casing and base trim; they are nailed to the bottom of the door jamb and the lower portion of the wall. When a door is trimmed with plinth blocks as well as decorative corner blocks, all the pieces meet with butt joints—there is no need for miters. Nail plinth and corner blocks in place with finishing nails long enough to penetrate well into the wall framing. Generally, 8d or 10d nails will do the job. Countersink the nails and fill the holes.

The door casing bottom butts into the top of the plinth block, while the base butts into its side. A plinth block should be slightly thicker than both the casing and the base. This allows it to conceal the end grain of those trim elements. The block should also be taller than the base for the same reason.

Installing Plinth Blocks. These decorative blocks provide a transition between casing and base.

Trimming Existing Door Casing

During the course of many re-modeling jobs, the old floor is buried beneath a new one. When the new floor is thicker than the old one, such as when hardwood or ceramic tile flooring is being added, the existing door casing can sometimes be a problem. The bottom of the casing must be trimmed. Unless you plan to replace the casing anyway, trim it in place rather than removing it. You can do this with a backsaw, or with a special saw designed for flush cutting. Once you know the thickness of the new floor, use a scrap of wood slightly thicker than the new floor, and use it as a guide for cutting all the door casings.

Exterior Details for Windows & Doors

There are several differences between exterior and interior window and door trim. Perhaps the most important difference is that exterior trim is not just there for appearance: it also helps to keep rain and wind from penetrating the walls. It is important that you use kiln-dried material. Otherwise, you'll get a lot of gaps at the joints from shrinkage, and the paint may fail as the trapped moisture tries to escape.

When installing exterior trim, take particular care to prevent water from penetrating joints. It is also a good idea to back-prime all trim before installing it, using a good-quality primer. This extra step will add years of life to the woodwork. If you plan to paint the trim and siding, be sure to caulk the joint between them well.

Caulking Windows & Doors

After installing any window or door trim, be sure to caulk the outside edges thoroughly between casing and siding. Use a high-quality, exterior-grade caulk. Caulk may be applied before or after the painting is complete. Be sure that the caulk fills the joint fully.

Exterior Details for Windows & Doors. The trim you choose conveys a particular style, as evidenced by the various treatments shown.

Installing Exterior Trim

Casing the outside of a door or window is not very different from casing the inside. The casing is set back from the edge of the jamb by a reveal, and head casing is installed with simple butt joints or, sometimes, miters. Galvanized casing nails secure the trim to the window jamb as well as to the wall.

Brick Mold. A type of casing that is unique to exterior work is called brick mold. This is a squarish molding with extra thickness to accommodate various thicknesses of siding. If the brick mold has a decorative edge, side pieces are mitered to the head piece.

Flat Trim. Flat trim, usually 1¼ inch thick, is commonly used for exterior casing in situations where brick mold is not used. It is sometimes called "five-quarter" trim. Flat trim is particularly appropriate when used with flanged windows and doors; it covers the flange. Some manufacturers recommend that you drill pilot holes through the trim and the flange for nailing purposes; others recommend that you avoid the flange altogether when nailing. Caulk the trim along both edges.

Drip-Cap Molding. This detail is not seen as much nowadays. It sits atop the head casing to deflect water away from that joint. It is nailed to the top of the casing with galvanized casing nails, then covered with metal flashing. A drip groove beneath the molding encourages water to drip clear of the jamb rather than seep between the drip cap and the jamb. One reason it is not used as much these days is that many windows feature integral flanges that serve as flashing.

Brick Mold. This casing is attached by manufacturers to the exterior edges of jambs.

Flat Trim. Use flat trim (sometimes called "five-quarter," or �, trim for its thickness) around flanged windows and doors.

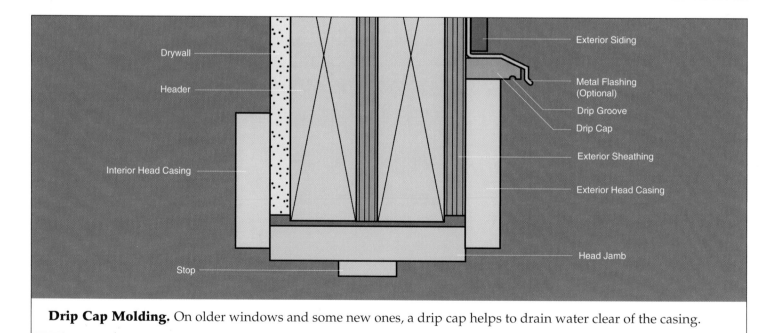

Drip Cap Molding. On older windows and some new ones, a drip cap helps to drain water clear of the casing.

final touches

Before Finishing

The last step in the installation of trim is to fill the holes left behind after setting all the nails. Though this is perhaps the easiest part of the job, it can readily turn into a headache of considerable proportions if you don't follow some simple guidelines.

What aggravates many beginners is the seemingly endless rounds of sanding, filling, and sanding again. It seems as though you're always reaching for the putty knife and wood filler to do a few more holes. The solution is simple: don't fill any nailholes until the entire job is complete and all the nails are set, or you'll loose track of which holes you've filled and which you haven't. There's nothing more frustrating than being up on a stepladder with a paint-laden brush, only to find several small holes that haven't been filled.

While you're filling holes, it's a good idea to scrutinize all the woodwork for small dents and rough areas—attending to them now will save lots of time later on. Dents can be filled with the same material used to fill nailholes; rough spots should be sanded smooth. Rather than try to see these flaws, feel for them. Rub your hand gently over all the trim, and you'll find more flaws than you could ever see. Another trick is to shine a strong light across the trim at a low angle; any irregularities will be accentuated by the shadows that they cast.

Filling a Hole

The key ingredient in filling holes goes by various names, including wood putty or wood filler. (Professional woodworkers use a product that's also called wood filler, but it is liquid and has nothing to do with filling holes.) Whatever you call it, the material is easy to use. Most formulations will accept various finishes, including varnishes and stains. Wood putty dries out quickly, however, so keep the container closed whenever you aren't actually dipping into it for more putty.

1. Filling. Choose a putty knife with a flexible, 1-inch blade. Scoop a small amount of putty out of the container; hold the knife at about a 30-degree angle; and force the putty into the hole with a swiping motion. Make another pass across the hole at a different angle to clear away any excess putty.

2. Inspecting. When the hole is filled properly, its edges can be seen clearly.

3. Finishing. After the putty dries (in as little as 15 minutes), you should sand it smooth. You can usually tell when putty has dried—it has a lighter color. Power sanding is generally unnecessary if the hole was filled properly; hand sanding does the job nicely.

1 — Putty Knife / Hole / Dab of Putty / First Swipe / Motion of Knife / Second Swipe

2 — Correctly Filled / Too Much Putty Left Behind

3 — Wood Block / Sandpaper

What to Avoid When Filling Holes

Filling holes is easy once you get the hang of it. After a while you may get so casual about it that you start to use your finger as a putty knife. Don't do it. As your finger passes over a hole, your skin will actually depress the top of the putty slightly, leaving a slight indentation that often can't be sanded flush with the wood surface. If you don't have a putty knife handy, an old credit card works nicely, too.

Another problem that beginners have is putting on too much putty (or, conversely, failing to scrape off enough). Wood putty dries hard as wood, and it's no easier to sand. Having excessive amounts of dried putty around a hole means only one thing: you'll need extra sandpaper and elbow grease to get rid of it. You'll find that it is much easier to remove putty before it dries.

Finishing Trim

Sanding. The wood used for trim is typically clear (that is, free of knots) and smooth. But sometimes you'll want to give it an extra going over with 100- or 120-grit sandpaper. The grain of the wood may have been raised slightly by contact with moisture, or perhaps you simply like the feel of ultra smooth wood. Sometimes the surface of trim is marred by marks left behind by the manufacturing machinery used to cut and shape it. These imperfections are called "mill marks" and can be removed by sanding as long as they aren't too extensive. In any case, trim with intricate details should be sanded by hand to keep the crisp edges from rounding over. But the flat portions of much trim can certainly be sanded mechanically. Three sanders appropriate for trim and related work are palm sanders, finishing sanders, and random-orbit sanders. When using any of these sanders, wear a dust mask, or connect a dust bag to the tool.

Painting. A good coat of paint, expertly applied, is the perfect finishing touch for any trim and molding. In addition, paint helps to protect the wood from wear and dirt.

Painting Tools

The standard paint roller used to apply paint to walls is hardly suitable for most trim. Its width makes it nearly impossible to maneuver through the intricate details of trim. There are, however, several varieties of trim rollers that can make quick work of intricate painting projects when used in conjunction with brushes.

A good brush, and the right one, is crucial. Disposable brushes are okay for modest touch-up work, but for high-quality trim painting you should invest in a high-quality brush. If you work mostly with oil-based paints, you will also need a supply of paint solvent for cleaning your brushes.

A Chinese bristle brush, made with natural animal hair, is best for applying oil-based paint, varnish, and stain. A synthetic brush is best for latex paint. Use a chisel-edge brush for painting edges; its angled bristles simplify the job. To use this brush, pull it so that the shorter bristles lead the longer ones, and work in long, steady strokes. A trim brush is ideal for reaching into intricate moldings, and it comes in various types of bristles to suit any paint.

Trim is most often finished with a gloss or semigloss paint. This makes it easier to clean than is possible with flat paint. It also makes a nice contrast with a wall that is painted with flat paint. There are several keys to a successful painting job.

■ Use long, steady strokes.

■ Apply the right amount of paint. Too much will blanket intricate details and leave runs behind; too little will lead to an uneven appearance.

■ Use paint shields or painting tape to protect adjacent surfaces. Painting tape is a wide paper tape with just enough tack along one edge to stay in place; it strips away much easier than standard masking tape.

Books have been written about the correct methods of painting, and continual improvements both in paint and painting tools make it difficult to generalize about this finish. Your best source of up-to-the-minute paint and painting advice is your local paint-supply store.

Sanding. Intricate moldings should be hand sanded; mechanical sanding can have the undesired effect of rounding the sharp edges.

- 100- or 120-Grit Sandpaper
- Base

Painting. Use painting tape to protect the wall when painting door trim.

- Painting Tape
- Chisel-Edge Paintbrush

Repairing Damaged Trim

If you know how to fill a nailhole, you can repair most of the damage likely to befall trim. Small dents, as well as holes left by removed hardware, are best repaired with wood filler. (See "Filling a Hole," page 72.)

You can also use wood filler to patch larger holes. Start by cleaning away any loose wood fibers or dust. Apply the filler in two passes, letting the first dry completely before applying the second. After the second layer is dry, sand it flush with the surrounding surface, using 100-grit paper. Hand sanding is best because the large area of filler will quickly clog sandpaper used in a power sander. If necessary, square up the edges of the patched area with a sharp chisel. Holes having an open edge, such as the mortise left behind after a hinge has been removed, can be repaired in similar fashion.

If you find that the damage is extensive and deeper than ⅛ inch or so, use an epoxy-based wood patch compound (which is available at hardware stores and home centers) or make a solid wood patch. The wood you use for a patch should match the existing wood as closely as possible.

1 **Cutting the Patch.** Cut an angular patch from some wood scrap. It should be large enough to cover all the damage and slightly thicker than the deepest part of the damage. Trace the shape of the patch on the wood.

2 **Routing the Patch.** Excavate the area by using a router fitted with a straight cutting bit or a wood chisel. Then clean up the corners of the excavation with the chisel.

Repairing Damaged Trim & Molding. To fill a shallow hole, spread putty in two layers.

3 **Gluing in the Patch.** Glue the patch in place. Once the glue has dried, sand the patch flush with the surrounding wood.

4 **Finishing the Patch.** Vacuum away all resulting sawdust, and then spread wood putty around the perimeter of the patch, forcing it into any gaps. After the putty dries, sand the area smooth.

1 The grain of the patch should run in the same direction as that around it.

2 Excavate the area to be patched using a router.

3 Glue the patch in place. Sand over it after the glue has dried.

4 Spread the wood putty around the perimeter of the patch.

Removing Base

1 **Removing Base Shoe.** First remove any molding, such as base shoe, that is attached to the baseboard. You may find that it's impossible to remove fragile base shoe molding without breaking it, but it is relatively inexpensive to replace. Slip a stiff paint scraper or (better yet) a small prybar behind the molding and pry it away from either the baseboard or floor. (You may have to experiment to figure out to which surface it is actually nailed, although it should be nailed to the base.)

2 **Pulling the Nails.** If you can't pry the molding loose with ease, drive the nails through the wood with a nail set and pull them after removing the molding; you can patch the holes later.

3 **Prying Base Loose.** Base is not nearly as flexible as molding, making it harder to remove but less likely to snap during the effort. Start at one end of the base, ideally where it intersects a door. (You can start at a corner, but make sure you don't try to loosen the butt end of a coped joint.) Then slip a prybar between base and wall, taking care not to damage the fragile top edge of the base or the wall. Slip a thin scrap of wood behind the prybar to protect the wall surface, and then gently lever the base away from the wall. Don't try to pull it entirely clear; you will crack the wood. Instead, continue down the length of the base with the prybar, opening up a modest gap as you work.

4 **Pulling Base Away from the Wall.** Then go back to where you started, open the gap a bit more, and again work your way down the base. Pry close to existing pairs of nails, rather than midway between them, for best results. The entire base trim should eventually pull away, along with all the nails.

1 Be careful not to apply too much pressure on the prybar or you will snap the molding.

2 If a molding will not pry loose, use a nail set to drive the nails through the wood before removing it.

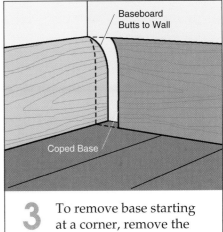

3 To remove base starting at a corner, remove the coped portion first, then the butt portion.

4 Pry the base away from the wall, getting as close to the pairs of nails as you can.

5 **Removing Base Using a Block and Hammer.** Another way to remove base is to pry it from the wall as just described, but once you've opened up a small gap, use a block and a hammer to pound the base trim back against the wall. Sometimes the nailheads will pop clear of the base, so you can pull them with the prybar.

6 **Wedging Base.** You can also remove base trim by wedging it away from the wall. Be sure to use a wood shingle or similar item as the wedge.

5 If the nailheads are visible, remove them one by one using a prybar; a scrap of wood will protect the base trim.

6 A wood shingle slipped behind the base trim works well to avoid damaging the wall.

Replacing Trim

You may be able to patch a length of trim, but sometimes nothing short of replacement will do. This is true if the damage is extensive, such as where rot or insect damage has had a long head start on a length of exterior corner trim. Another reason to replace trim is to avoid a time-consuming process of stripping layers of paint that have accumulated over the years.

Before replacing any trim, however, ask yourself a few questions before you reach for your tools:

■ Is the trim old? If so, you may not be able to match adjoining trim exactly in width and profile. This might not be a problem if all the casing in a room is going to be replaced, however.

■ Is the trim made of hardwood? Hardwood trim commands a premium price, so you face considerable

expense if you plan to replace your old hardwood with new hardwood. This is a case where even a big stripping job may be worth the effort. If the wood is painted, scrape a small portion of the paint away from an unobtrusive place to see the bare wood.

■ Is the trim curved? Replacing the curved head casing over an arch-top window can be expensive and time consuming, and usually justifies the effort spent repairing damage.

Caution: Stripping paint when remodeling can be a health hazard. Older paints may contain lead, and sanding them releases lead-laden dust into the air. Such dust can be highly toxic, particularly to children. Always have your paint tested for lead before removal if your house was built prior to the 1980s.

Removing Door & Window Casing

You can often remove casing just as you would base trim—by gradually prying it loose with a prybar. But you may find a need for additional techniques, particularly when it comes to removing exterior trim. That's because exterior trim is thicker (typically 1¼ inch thick) and wider than interior trim and may be held with galvanized nails, which won't give up without a fight.

Cutting Nails. If you can't pry the casing loose, you may be able to cut the nails instead, particularly when it comes to door and window trim. Slip a hacksaw blade between trim and jamb to cut through each nail shank. After removing the casing, you can either extract the remaining shanks with nippers or simply pound them farther into the jamb.

Removing Assembly Nails. Cornerboards are usually nailed together before they're nailed to the wall, so you may have to cut the assembly nails before you can pry each board away from the wall. It may

When you remove trim, there's a good chance that the nails will still be attached. If you aren't going to reuse the wood, bend back the nails to minimize any accidental scratch or puncture wounds, and dispose of the trim promptly. If you plan to reuse the wood, the best way to remove nails is to pull them through the wood from the back side using nippers or side cutters. Pounding them back through the wood is likely to splinter it, and exposes a hole that has to be patched. Grasp the shank of the nail with one edge of the nippers, and lever the nail out.

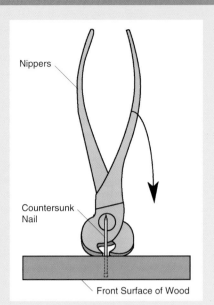

be easiest to drive the assembly nails through the top piece using a nail set.

Pulling Nails. Another way to remove trim, particularly if you can't reuse it anyway, is by driving the claws of a cat's paw nail puller into the wood to reach the head of a countersunk nail.

Place the tip of the cat's paw over a

nailhead. Strike the back of the tool with a hammer to drive the nail-pulling claw at an angle into the wood; you may have to try several times. Then use the tool as a lever to remove the nail. This will result in some damage to the wood, so use this technique only if you plan to replace the removed trim with new trim.

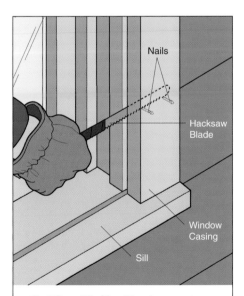

Cutting Nails. Use heavy tape or a plastic handle to protect your hands from the hacksaw blade, and wear gloves as well.

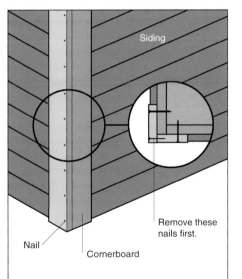

Removing Assembly Nails. To remove assembly nails, drive them through the top piece of wood with a nail set or use a hacksaw to cut them.

Pulling Nails. A cat's paw driven into the wood enables you to remove nails that have been countersunk.

5 Final Touches

Recognizing Rot & Insect Damage

Relentless cycles of wetting and drying, 100-degree temperature swings, the corrosive effect of salt air—the environment outside of a house is a tough place for any material. Wood, however, has additional enemies, including insects and fungi. (A fungus is essentially a plant with no leaves that gets nutrients from organic matter such as wood.) Trim used indoors is unlikely to be attacked, but outdoors the story is different. Likely locations for problems include anywhere wood is close to the ground, including the bottoms of door casing and corner-boards, skirt boards, and any trim around decks.

Prevention and Diagnosis. Wood-destroying fungi and insects all require about the same basic conditions to thrive, though in various measures: oxygen, favorable temperatures, a food source, and moisture. If you eliminate any of these essentials, you make it that much more difficult for the organism to survive. Of these factors, it's generally easiest to remove the source of moisture by caulking joints, keeping wood well away from earth contact, and ensuring proper ventilation. Chemical treatments of wood can remove it as a food source, so you can use pressure-treated wood where it must touch or be close to the ground.

There are several ways to determine whether you might have a problem. You may be able to see the clues, but if not, tap the wood with a hammer and listen for the dull thud indicating interior damage. If you can stick a standard screwdriver even partway into the wood without much effort, the wood may be infested with insects or fungi. Call in a professional to determine the best course of treatment.

Enemies of Wood

Name	Damage	How to Recognize
Brown rot	Strength of wood decreases rapidly. Most common fungi in houses.	Wood dark brown and crumbly; breaks into small cubical pieces.
White rot	Strength of wood decreases slowly. Most common on hardwoods.	Wood looks bleached, feels spongy, has black lines running throughout the bleached area.
Soft rot	Wood softens increasingly from surface inward. Occurs where wood is exposed to moisture for long periods.	Similar to brown rot.
Mold	Doesn't harm wood directly, but increases moisture permeability of wood that encourages growth of decay fungi.	Darkened areas on the wood surface, often black, green, or yellow. If discolored wood feels dry, fungus is probably inactive. Can grow on or through a paint film. Most likely on shaded portion of house. Staining can be removed by bleaching or light sanding.
Subterranean termite	Most destructive insect. Feeds on cellulose in wood, but damage is difficult to see from surface even when infestation is severe.	Nest in the ground but will travel up to 40 yards to a feeding source. Most common sign of infestation is a swarm of winged termites congregating on portion of house. Also look for feeding tubes that lead from ground to wood.
Carpenter ant	Does not eat wood, but tunnels through rotted or rotting wood while nesting.	Look for swarming outdoors in spring or indoors any time. Look for small piles of sawdust near infestation.
Powderpost beetle	Attacks only hardwoods. Oak firewood is a common source of indoor infestation.	Leaves small, extremely fine piles of sawdust near infested wood. Attracted to light, so may be found on window sills in infested rooms. Leaves small holes that look as if drilled with $\frac{1}{32}$ to $\frac{1}{16}$-inch drill bit.

glossary

Apron The piece of trim at the bottom of a window, below the stool.

Back band Molding used to decorate the outer edges of flat casing. It can also be used as a base cap.

Base cap Molding applied to the top of base trim.

Base shoe Molding used to conceal any variation between the floor and base bottom. It is also used to cover edges of sheet vinyl flooring (when installed without first removing base trim).

Base trim Sometimes called base molding, base trim protects the lower portion of the walls and covers any gaps between the wall and the floor.

Biscuits Football-shaped pieces of compressed wood glued into slots that have been cut into the pieces of stock that will form a joint.

Blocking Wood stock toenailed between or adjacent to studs to give you a solid surface into which to nail the molding.

Built-up trim Several profiles of trim combined to appear as one large piece of molding. Most often it is used as ceiling trim or on the exterior of the home.

Butt joint Two pieces of wood joined at their square cut ends.

Casing The trim that is used to line the inside and outside of a doorway or window frame.

Chair rail Molding installed at a height that protects walls from being damaged by chair backs. It is also used to cover the edges of wainscoting.

Clear grade A grade of lumber or trim that has no knots or other visible defects.

Compound miter A cut that angles in two directions simultaneously.

Coped cut Made with a coping saw, a curved cut is made on a piece of molding with a 45-degree mitered face.

Coped joint A curved cut made across the grain of molding that makes a reverse image of the piece against which it must butt.

Corner guard Trim that protects the outside corners of drywall or plaster in high-traffic areas.

Cove Molding that covers the inside corners between sheets of paneling. It is also used for built-up crown molding.

Crosscut A straight cut that runs across the grain of the wood. Because the grain of trim runs along the length of the piece, a crosscut would be made across the width of the trim.

Crown Molding that is used for a dramatic effect at the juncture of walls and ceilings.

Half-lap miter joint A joint that combines miter, cope, and butt cuts. Half-lap miters are used for moldings with full, rounded-over tops.

Jamb The inside surfaces of a window or door opening.

Miter cut A straight cross-grain cut made at an angle other than 90 degrees to join two pieces of wood.

Mitered return Used to continue the profile of trim back to the wall when the trim does not meet another piece of trim.

Miter joint A corner joint formed by cutting the ends of two pieces of lumber at an equal angle—often 45 degrees.

Molding Thin strips of wood that have a profile created by cutting and shaping.

Mullion casing Center trim that is used between two or more closely spaced windows.

Paint-grade trim Trim made of many small pieces of wood joined together into one long piece, using glue and interlocking joinery called finger joints.

Picture molding Molding used to hang metal hooks to suspend paintings and wall hangings, so there is no need to put holes in the wall.

Plumb Vertically straight, in relation to horizontally level surface.

Reveal Amount of the jamb (usually ⅛ to 3/16 inch) that is allowed to show at the edges of the casing of a window or door.

Rigid polyurethane molding Trim that is extruded into various profiles and sizes. It is lightweight, stable, and paintable.

S4S Stands for "surfaced four sides." Designates dimension lumber that has been planed on all sides.

Sash The framework into which window glass is set. Double-hung windows have an upper and a lower sash.

Scarf joint A 45-degree miter cut across the grain that is used to join lengths of trim end to end.

Screen molding Half-round or flat molding used to protect the cut edges of screening nailed to a wood screen door.

Shelf edging Trim that covers the exposed edges of plywood or particleboard casework and shelving.

Shims Thin wood wedges (often cedar shingles) used for tightening the fit between pieces, such as filling the gap between the window frame and rough-opening sill when installing a window.

Stool The piece of window trim that provides a stop for a lower sash and extends the sill into the room.

Stops Narrow strips of wood nailed to the head and side jambs of doors and windows to prevent a door from swinging too far when it closes and to keep the window sash in line.

Stud Vertical member of a frame wall, usually placed at each end and every 16 inches on center.

Trim General term for any wood used in a house that is not structural lumber. Also, ornamental enhancements that improve the appearance of buildings, both exterior and interior. Includes plain and shaped members.

Wainscoting cap Molding used to cover the exposed end grain on solid or paneled wood wainscoting.

Wainscoting Paneling, paint, fabric wallcovering or other material applied to the lower half of an interior wall.

index